The Art of Robin Bolton

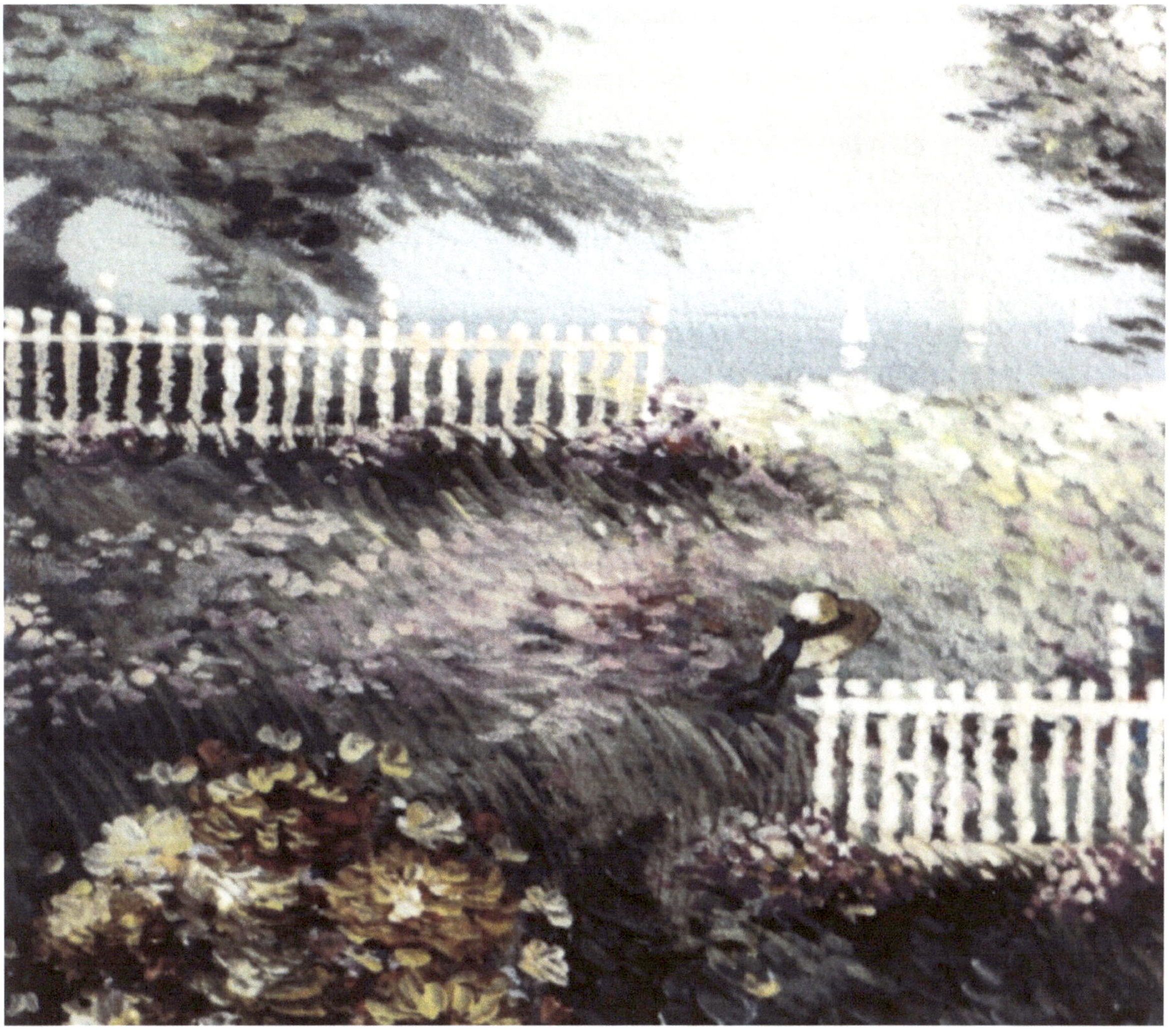

Poetry & Compilation by J. S. Friday

2020

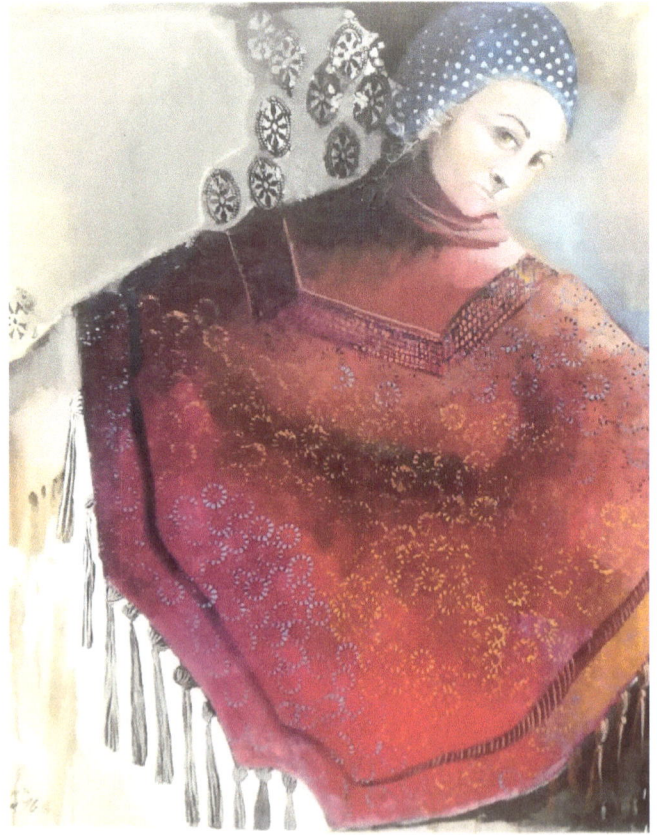

Cover Art: self portrait of Robin R Bolton dated & signed 1976.

Signed by Robins brush:

Robin Ricketson ©

Robin R. Bolton ©

Robin Ricketson Bolton ©

Robin Bolton ©

R. Bolton ©

Contents

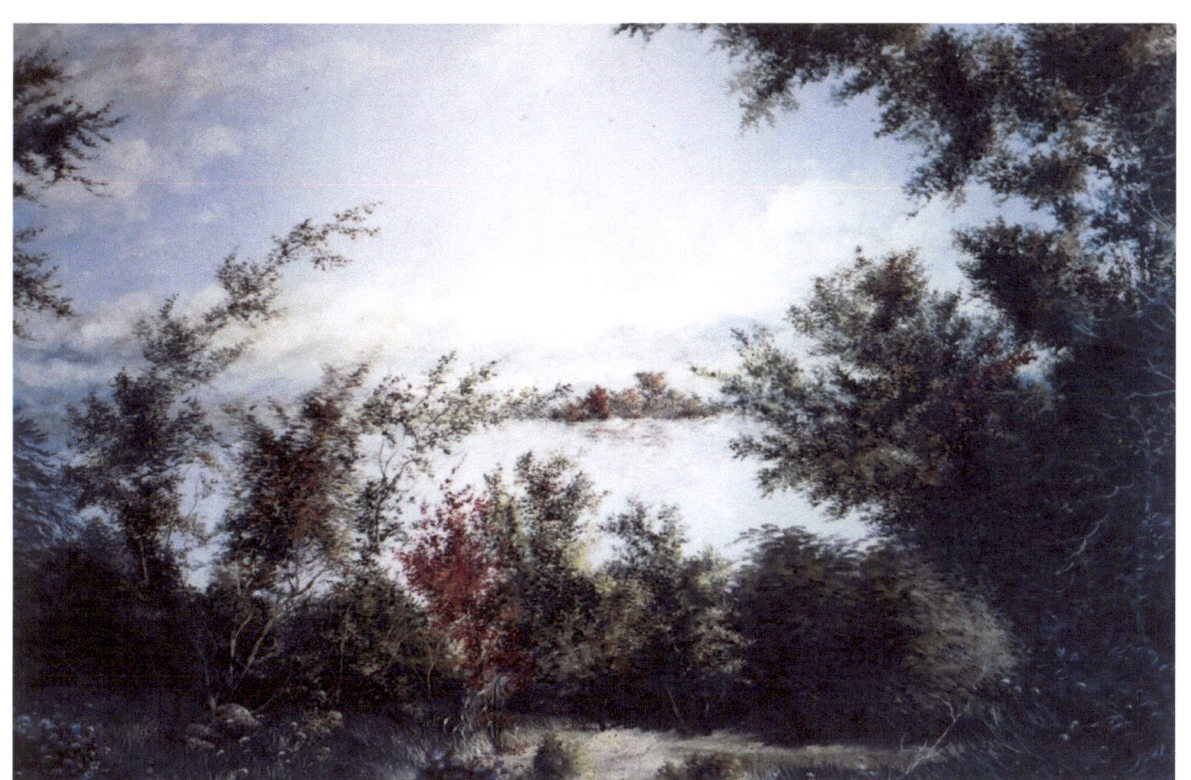

Lake Burton from a Distance

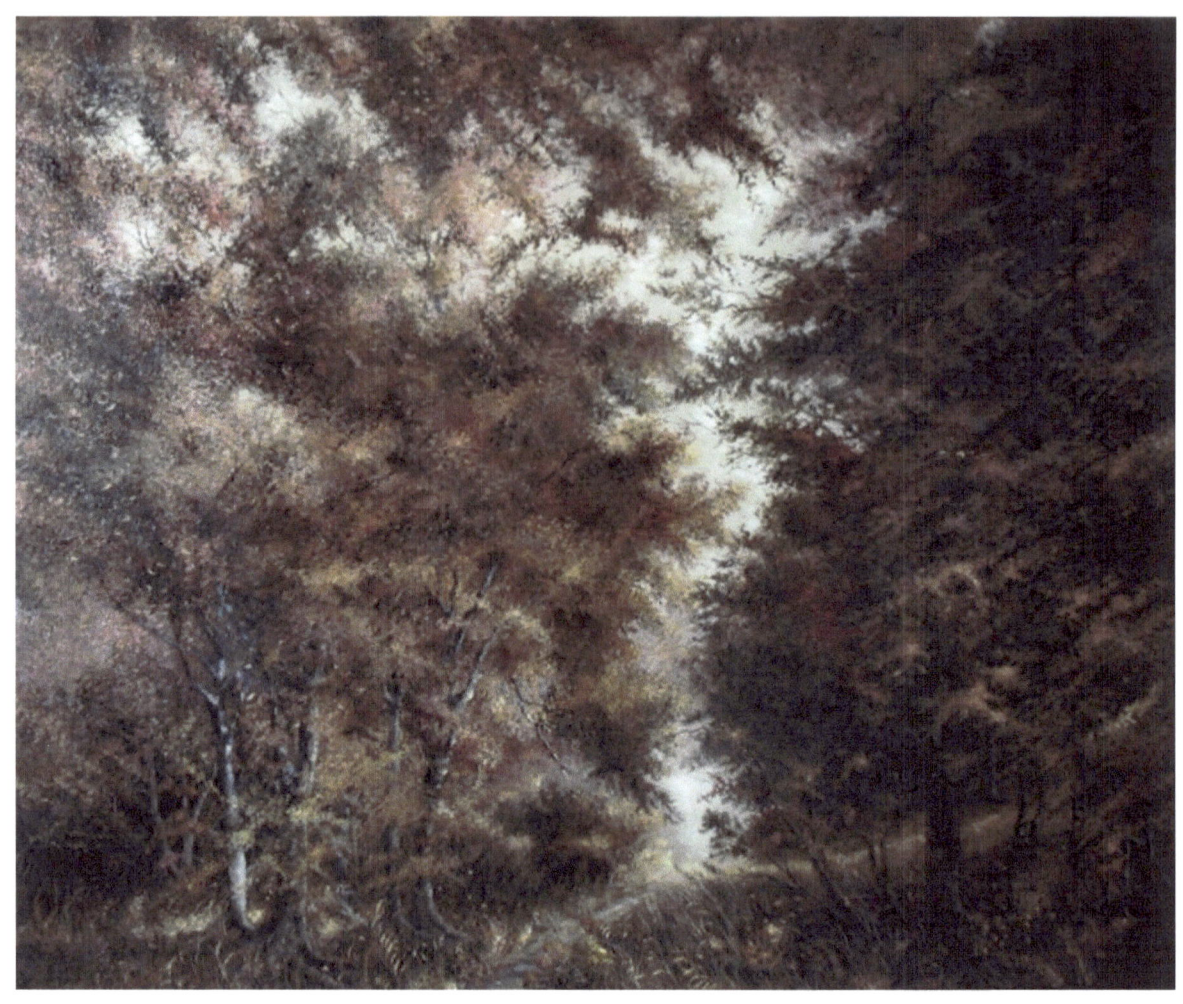

Autumn Melody

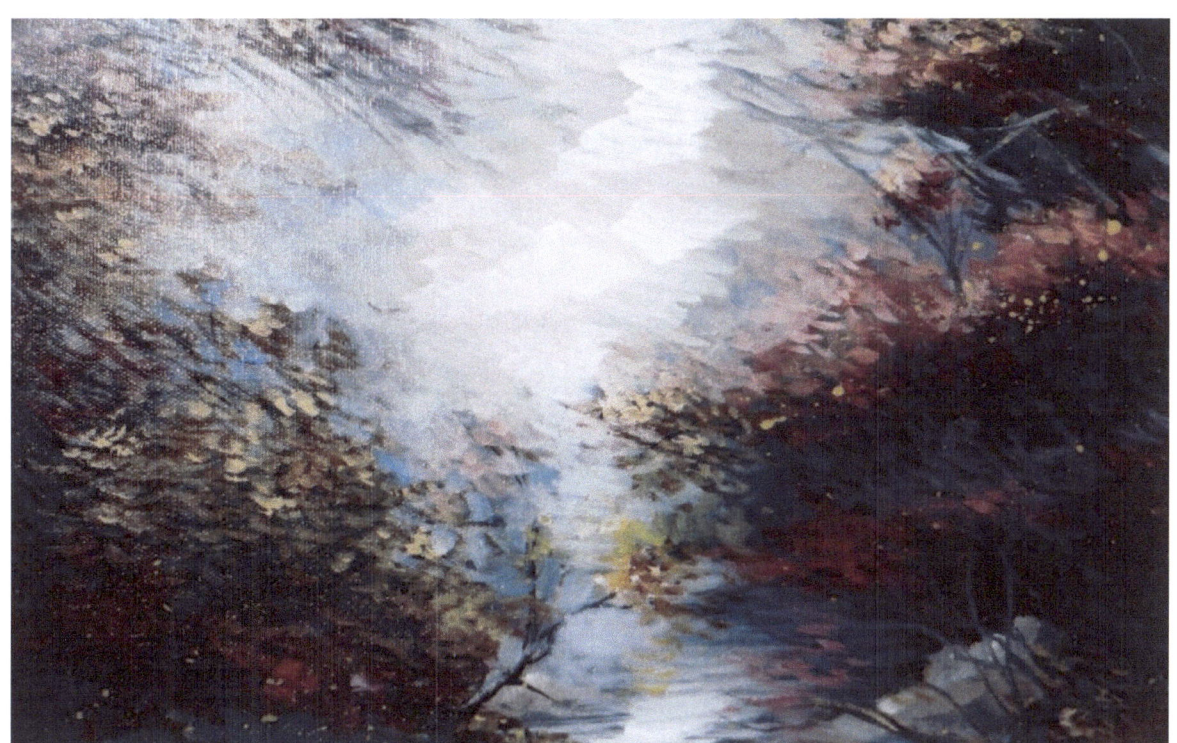

Trail of Colour

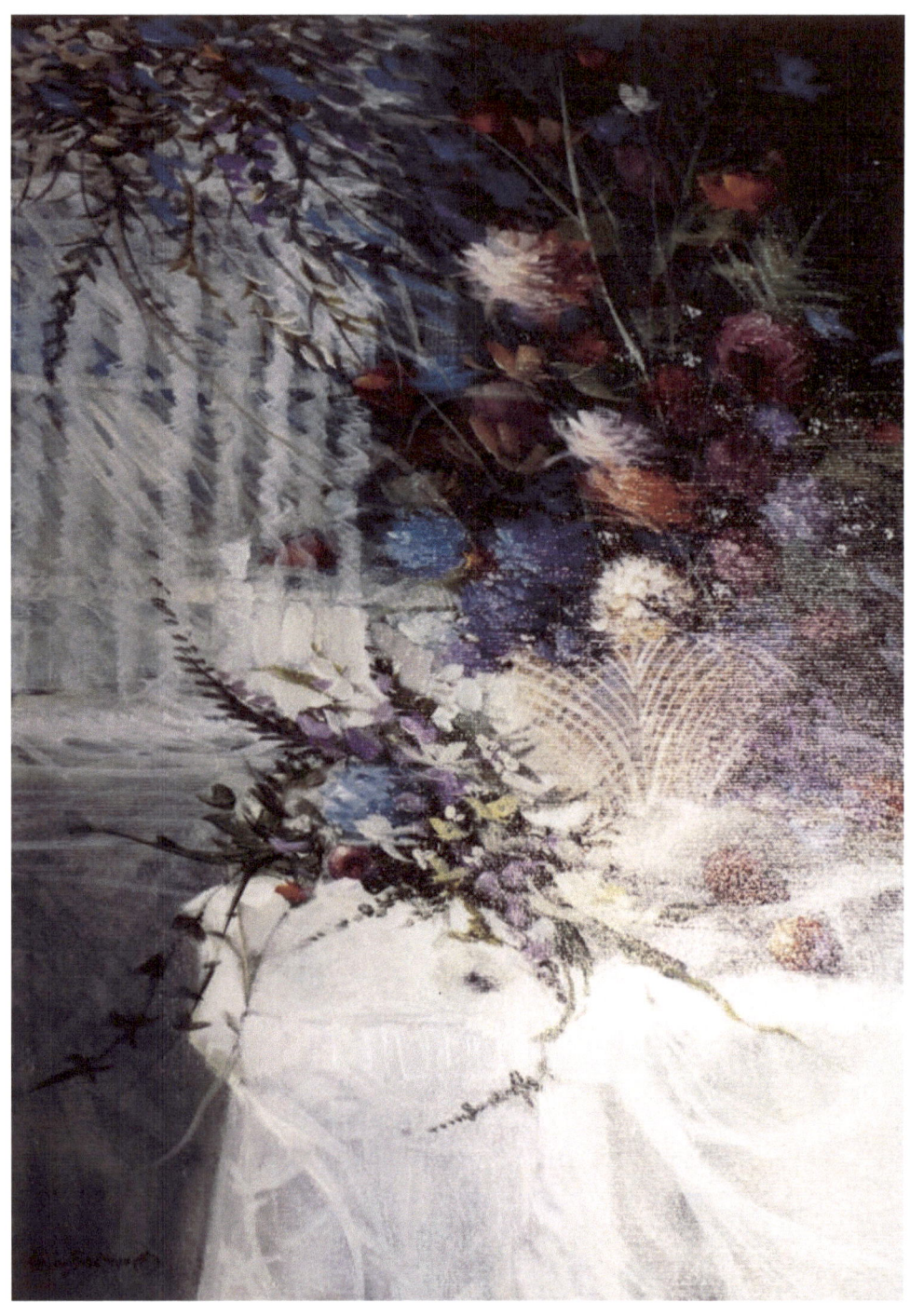

Victorian Porch Bouquet

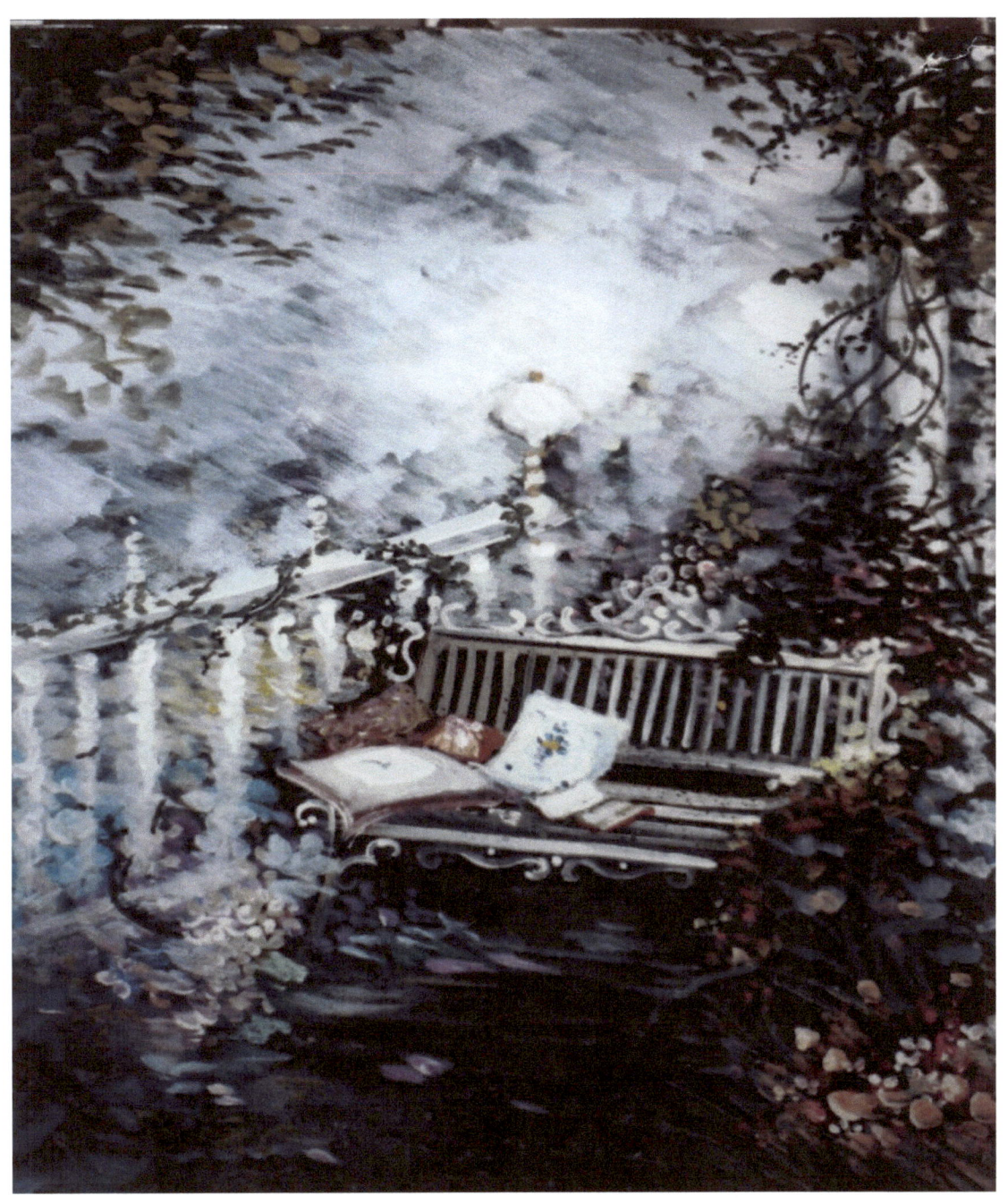

Front Porch Library

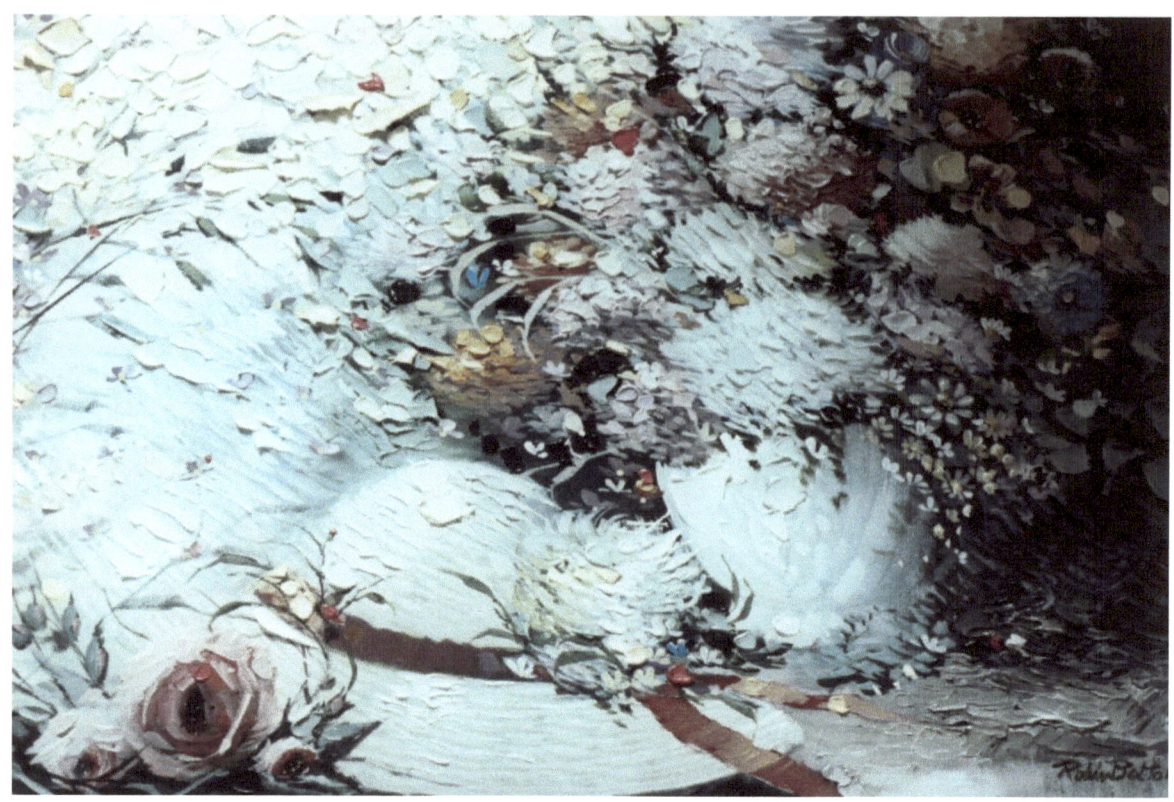

Hat & Flower - Combination

Gardenia -

Cape Jasmine, a popular wedding flower
known for its silk petals, fragrance and beauty
a scented green plant, but won't overpower
Cape Jasmine, a popular wedding flower
can accent candles and the church tower
buy them locally, so you don't pay a duty
Cape Jasmine, a popular wedding flower
known for its silk petals, fragrance and beauty.

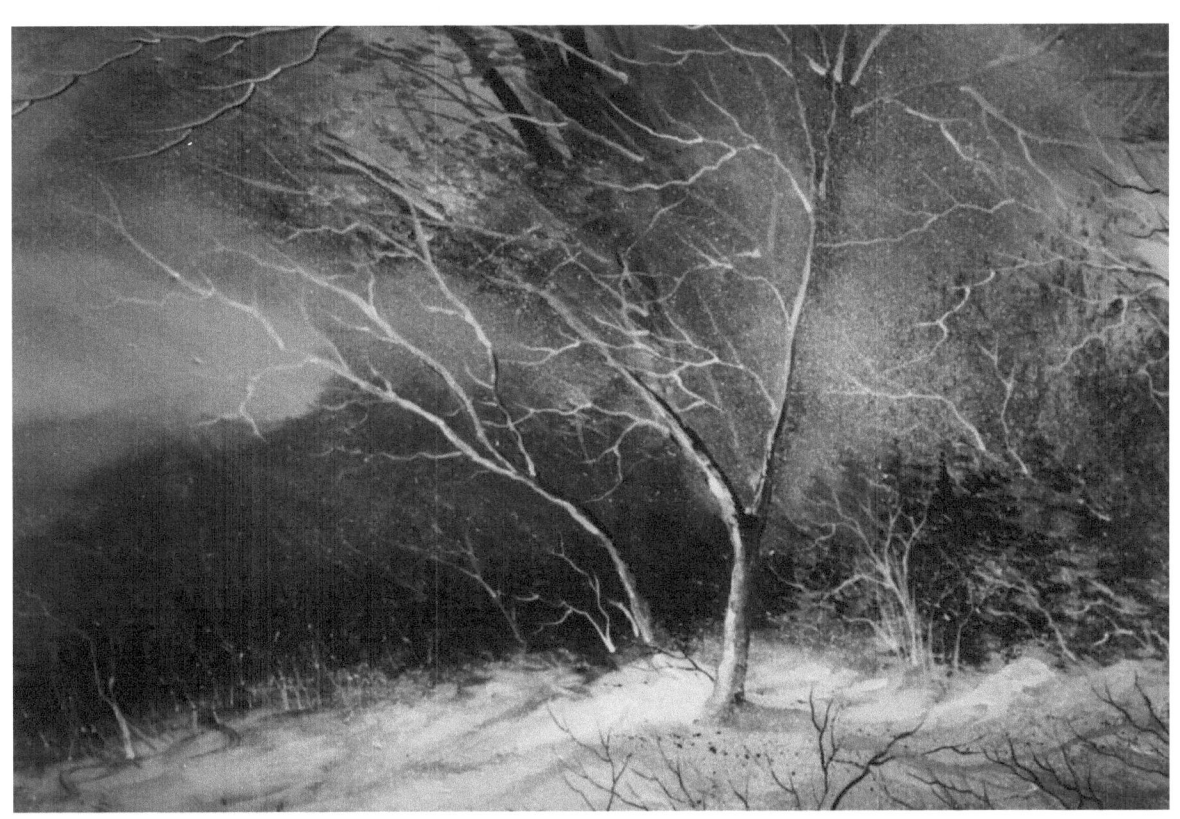

Snow across the Mountains

4ft X 5 ft

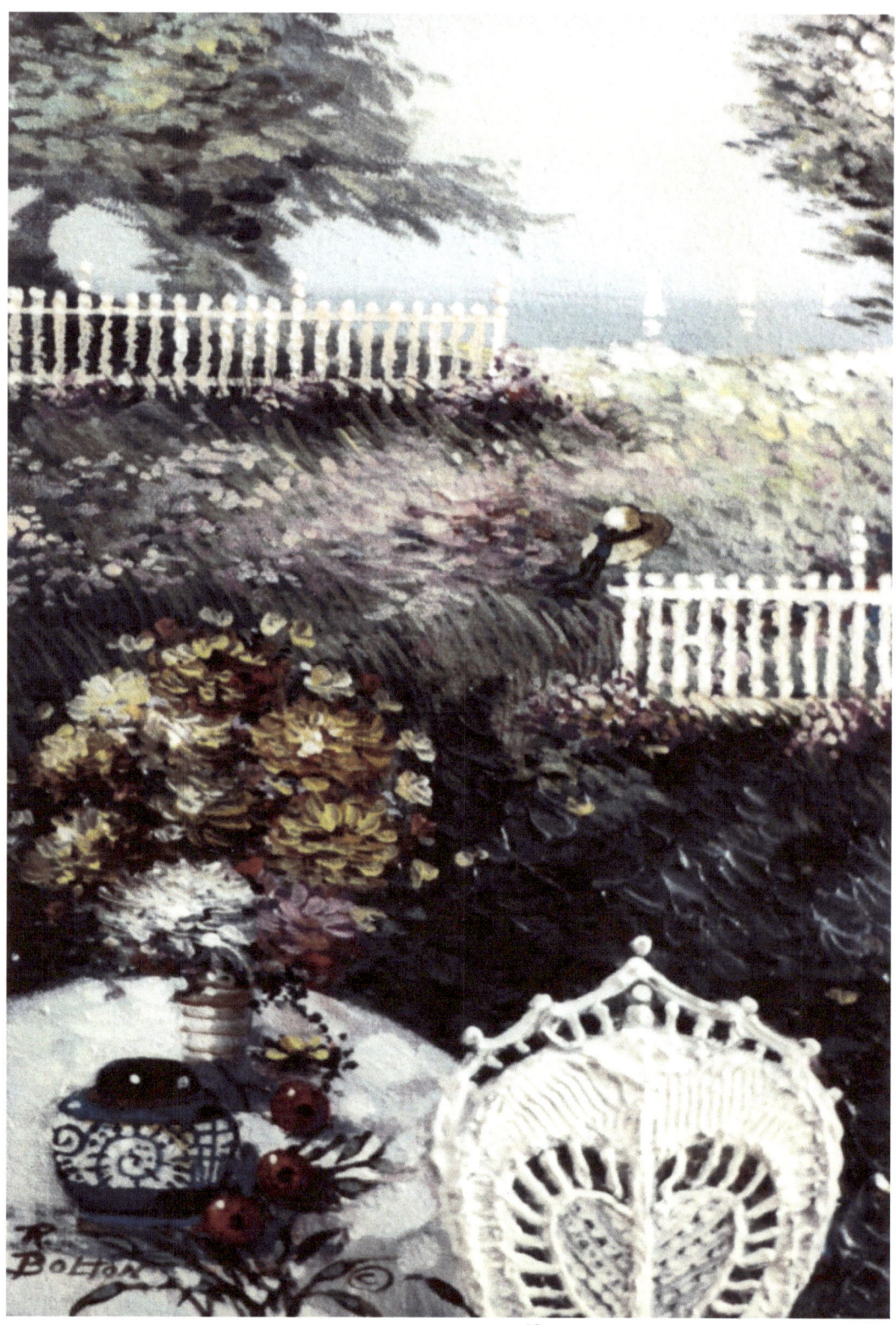

Cape Cod

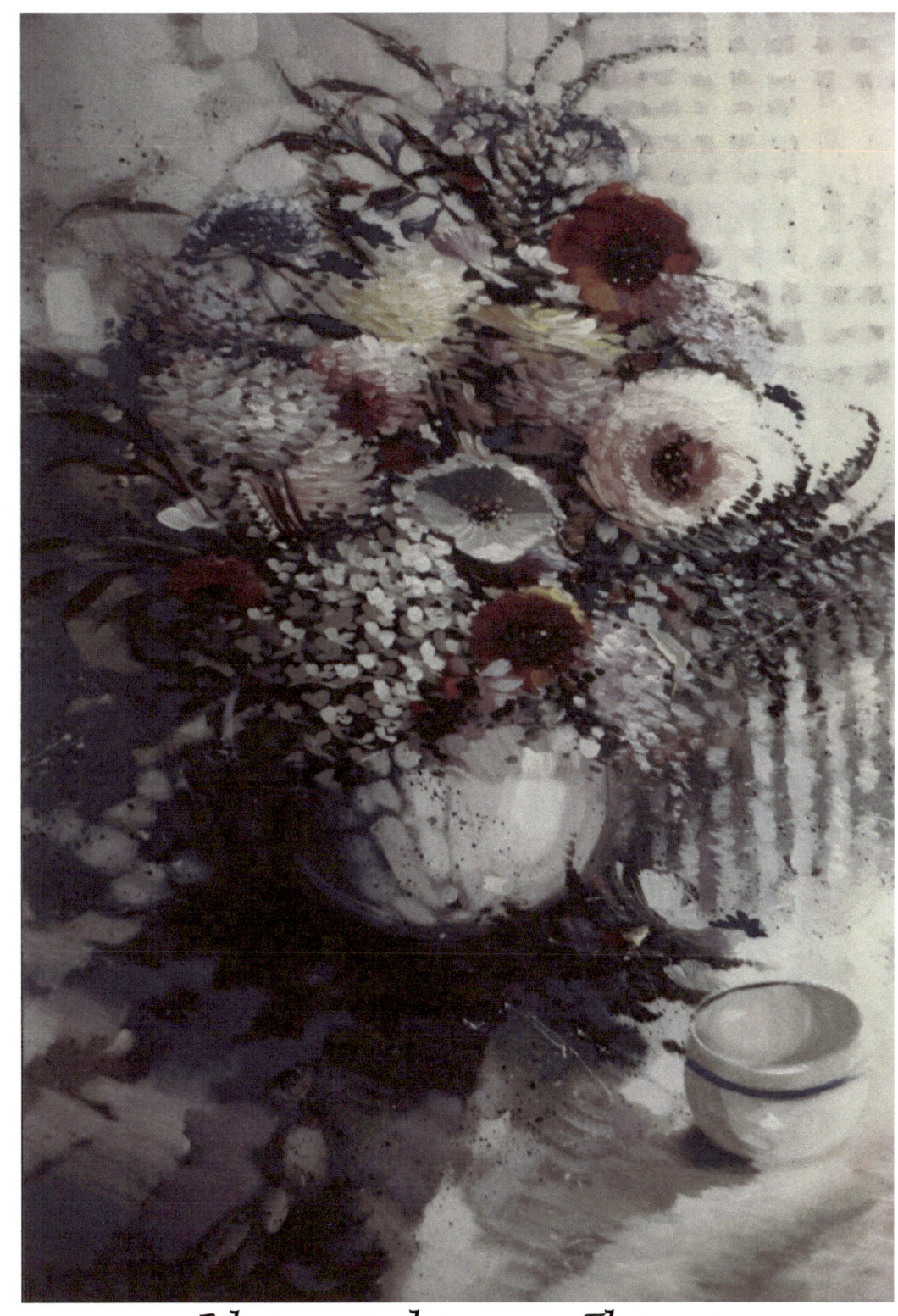

I love you honey....Flowers

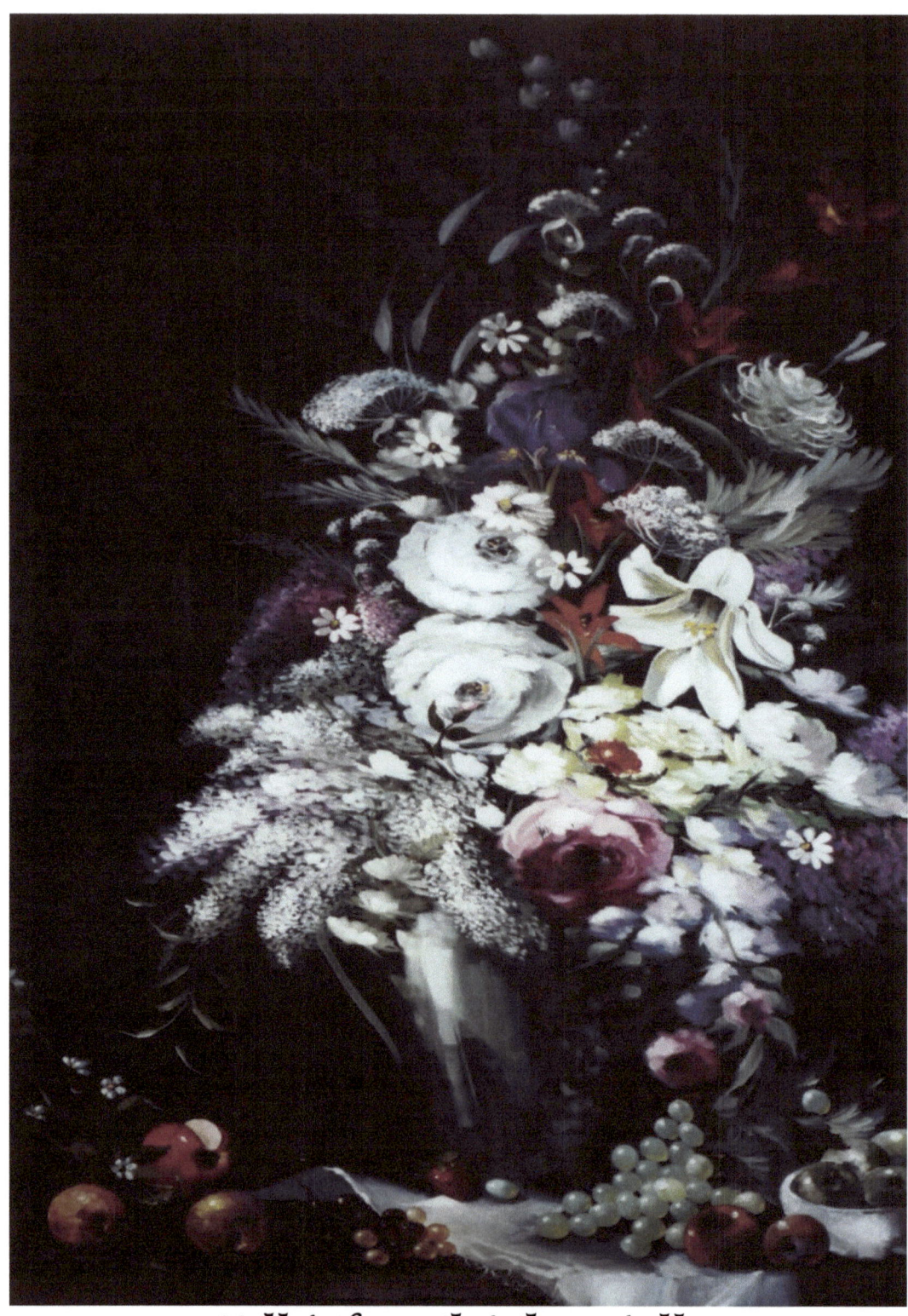

Still Life with White Lilly

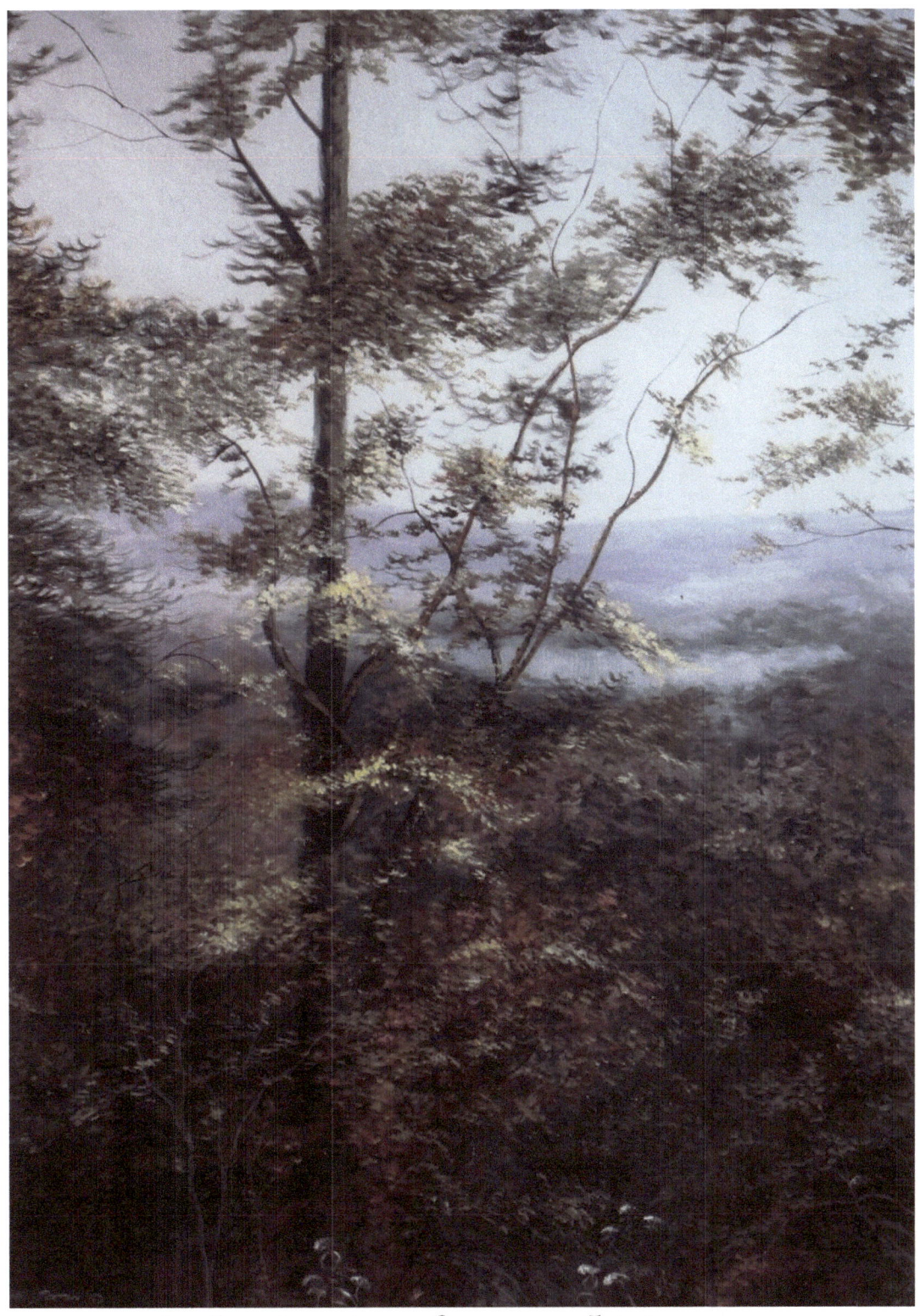

Lake Burton from a distance..

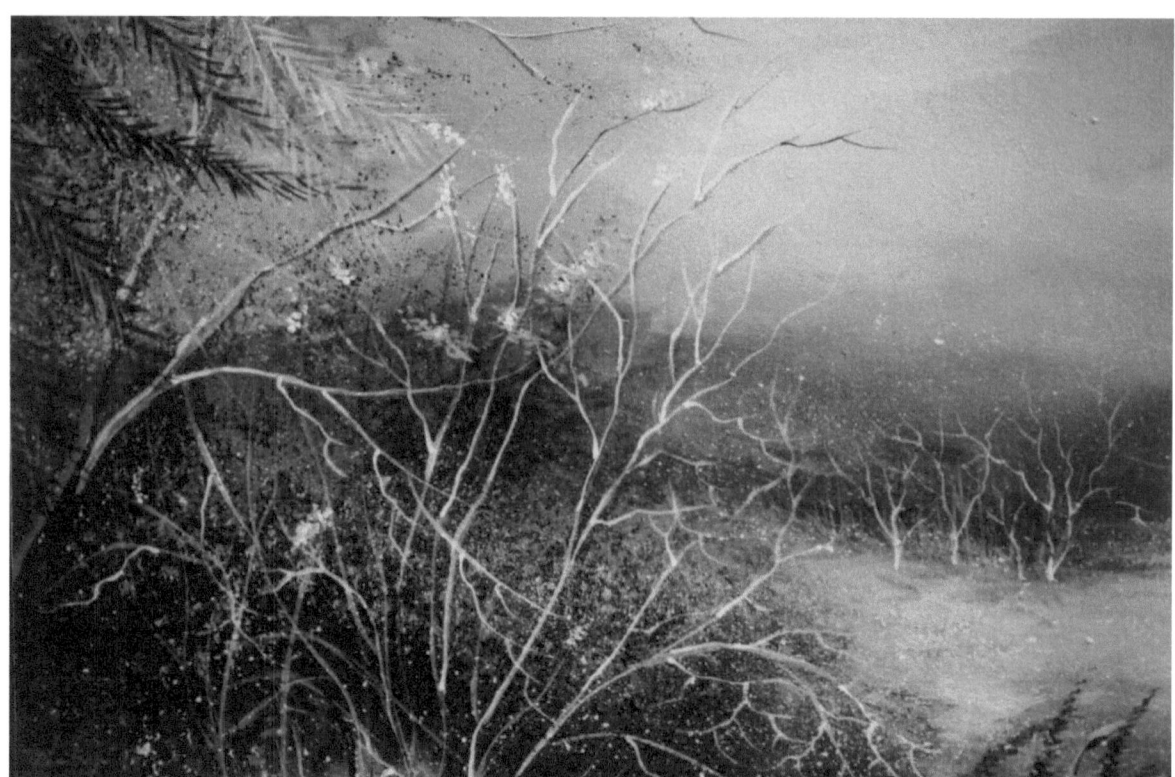

Wintery Outlook

Permafrost –

Grazing on the plains
permafrost desolate snow
waiting for the melt.

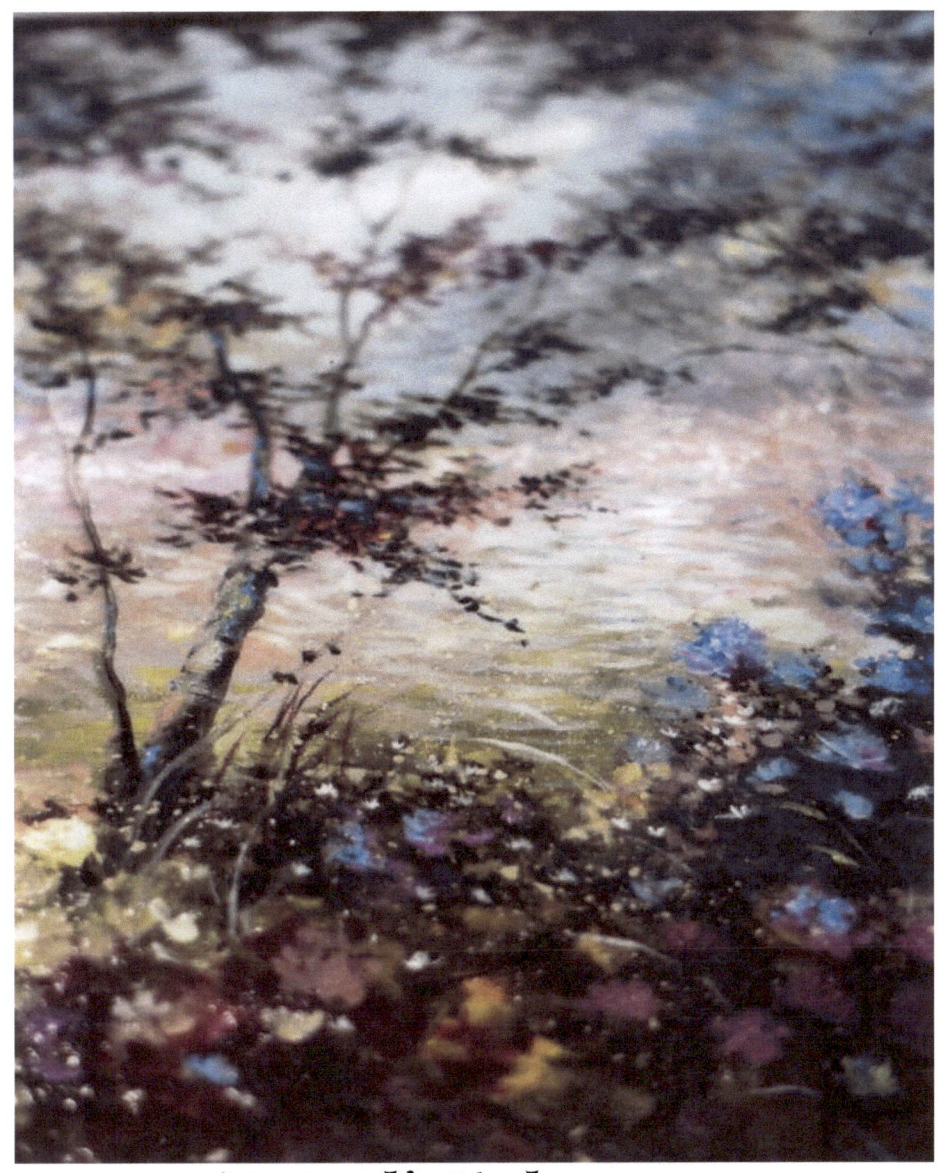

My Dad's Hydrangeas
11x14

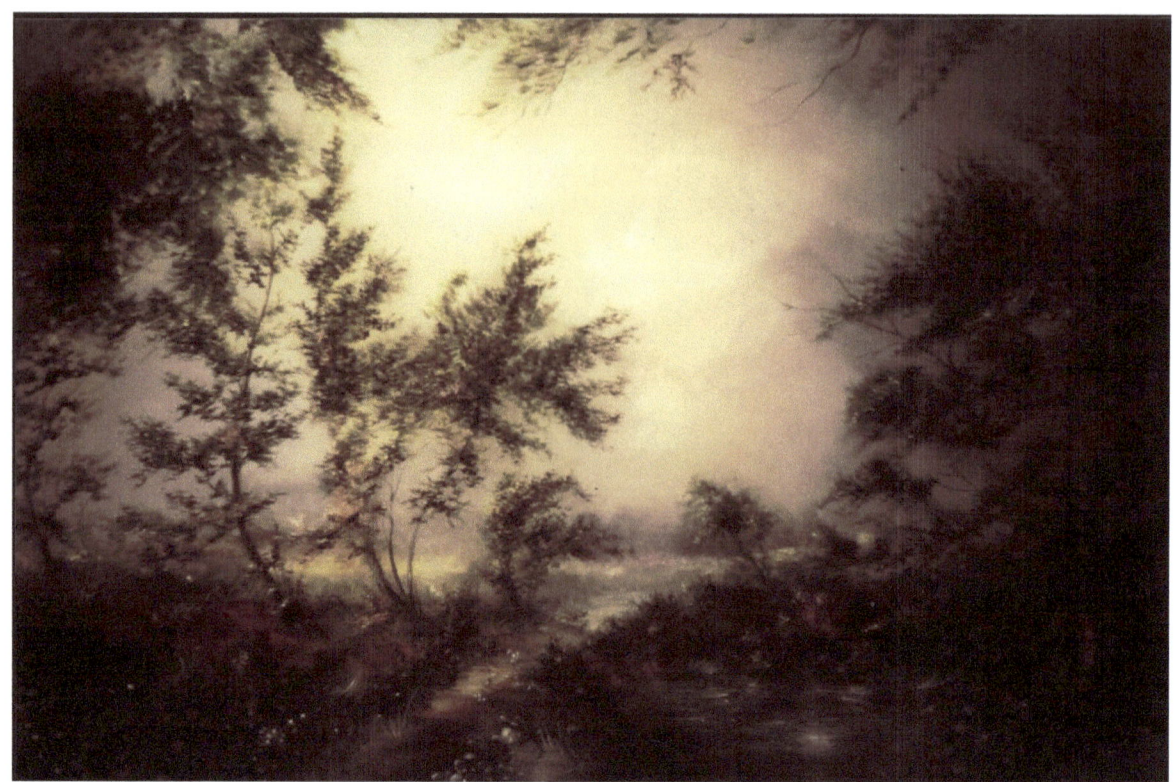

Moment in Time..

Monumental Trees ~
Colossal Green Tree
pass throughout epochs of time
shading visitors.

Georgia Mountains ~
Dark becomes the land
shadow creatures are at hand
Last beacon of light.

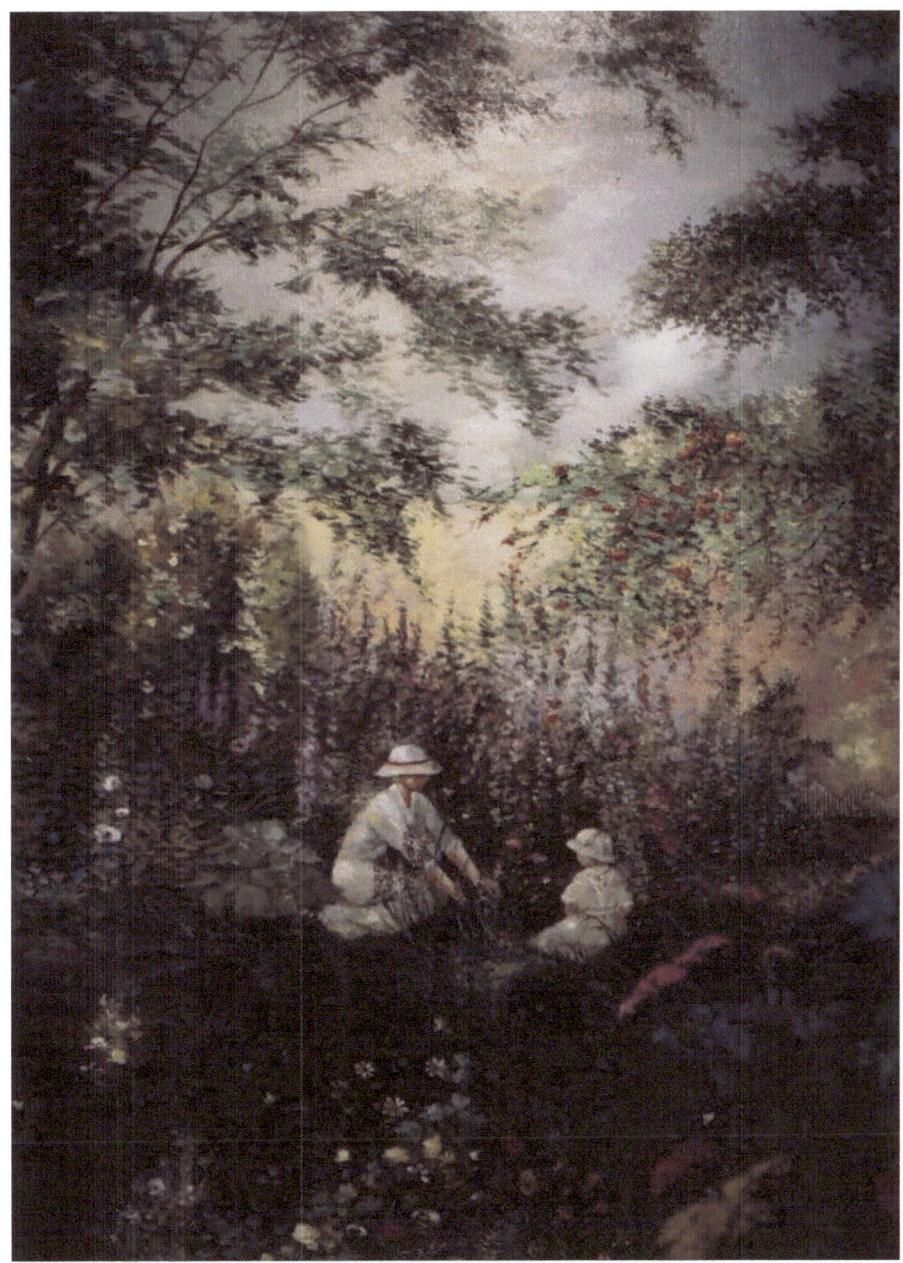

Laura Jean's Garden

Rush to the Garden ~
A Strawberry
which grew from a white bloom and vine.
A Strawberry
which was hand grown in Auberry;
like a red perennial wine.
whose bouquet smells so sweet and fine,
A Strawberry.

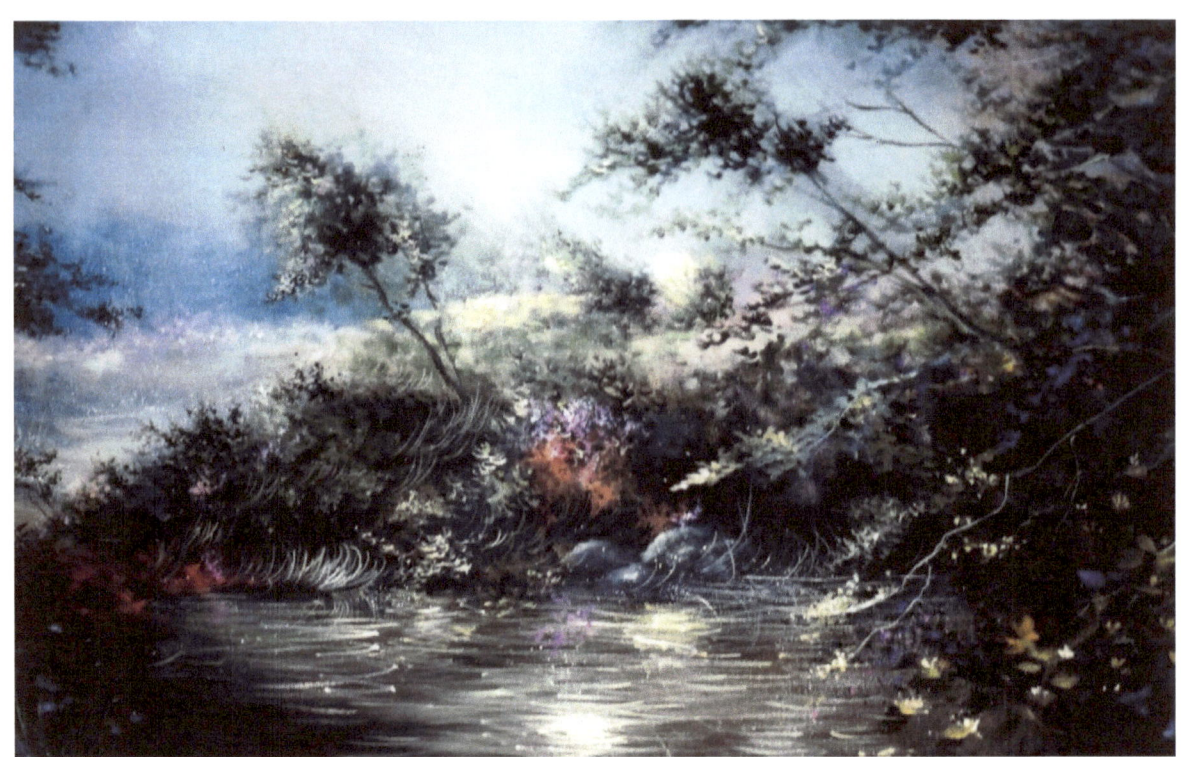

Spring Mist ' Rabun County

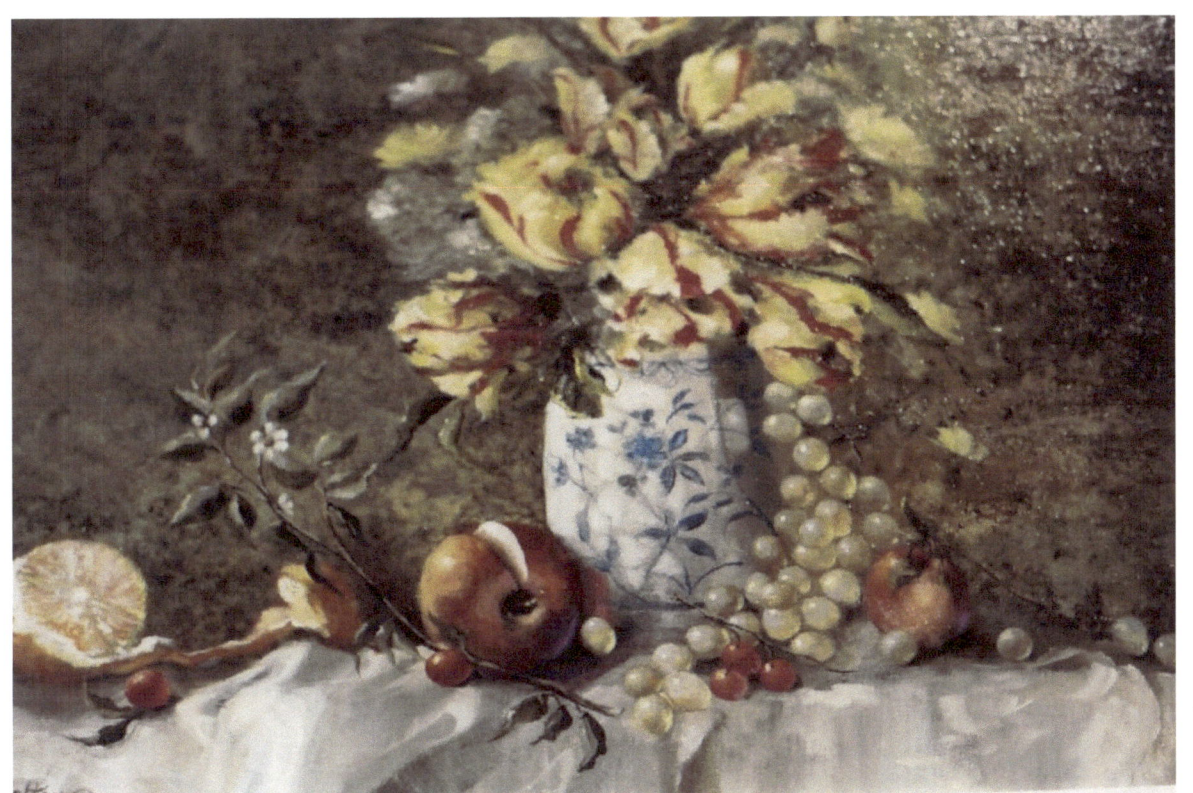

Still Life with Tulips
16x20

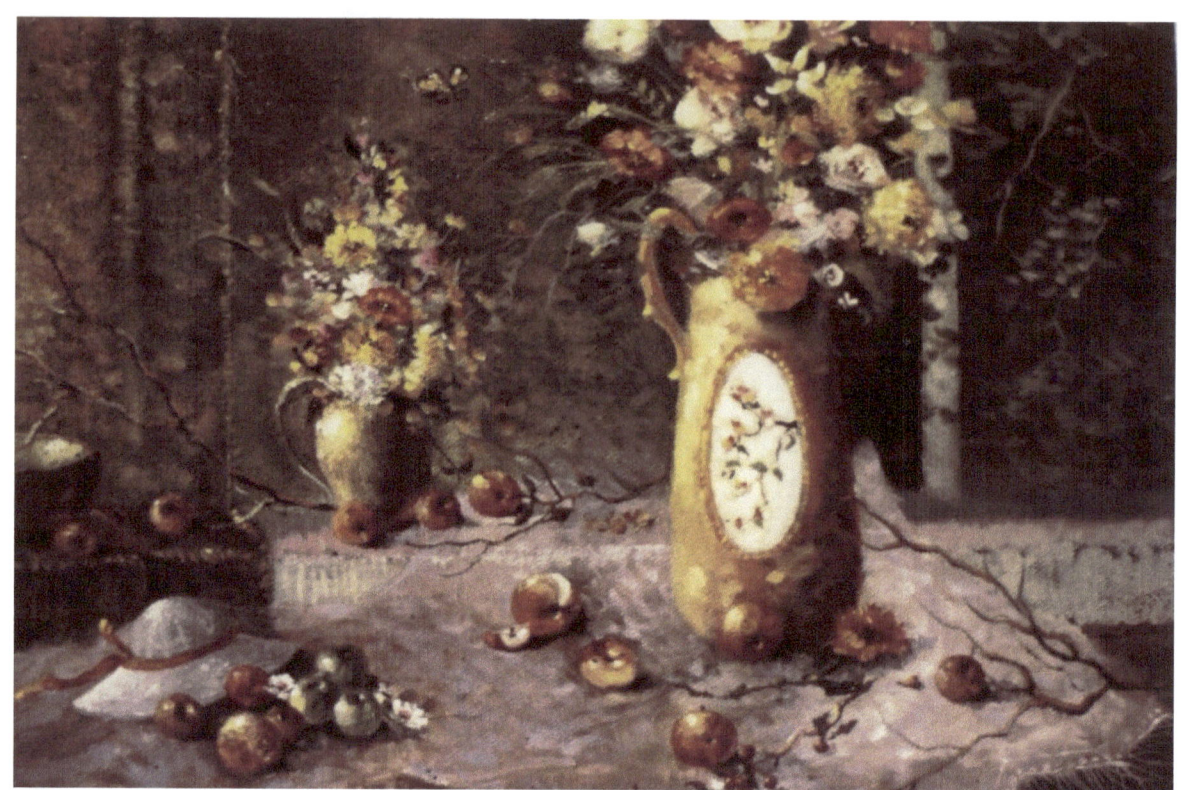

Still life with Butterfly

11x14

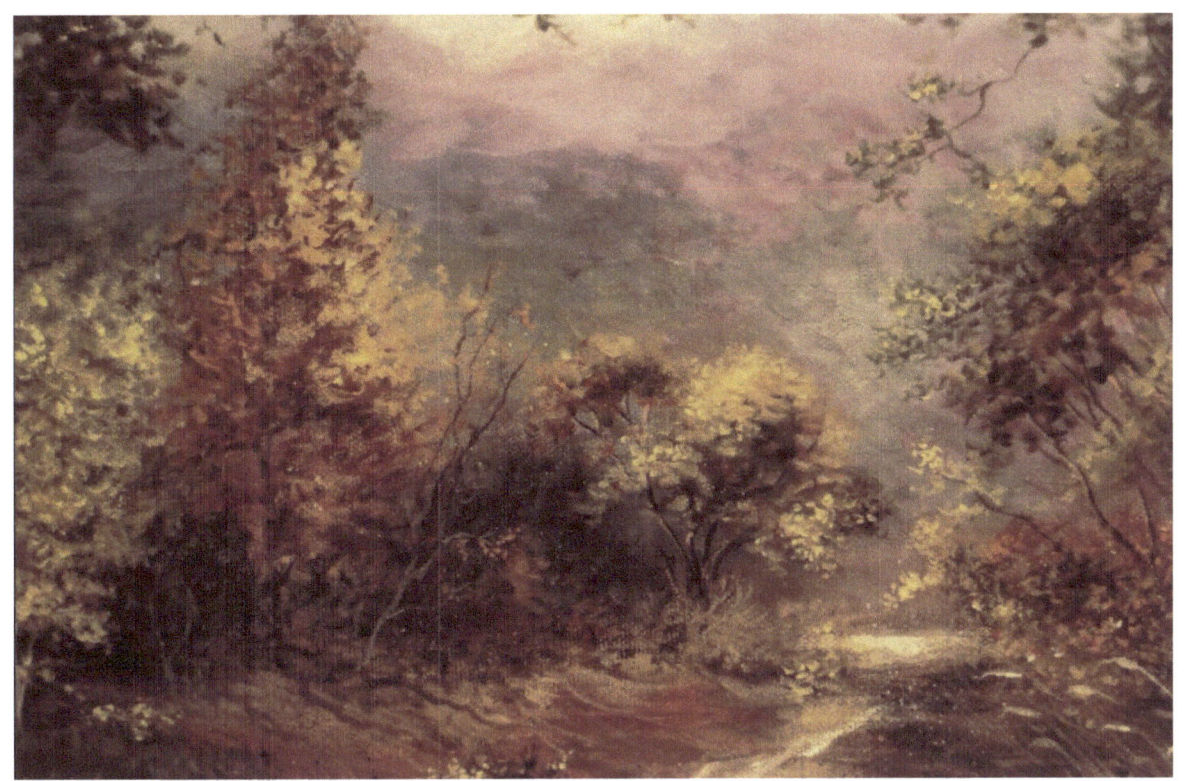

Golden Brilliance
11x14

Fall Reflections –

Crisp and Clear, Fall starts
Carmine and Orange swagger
lake colors reflect.

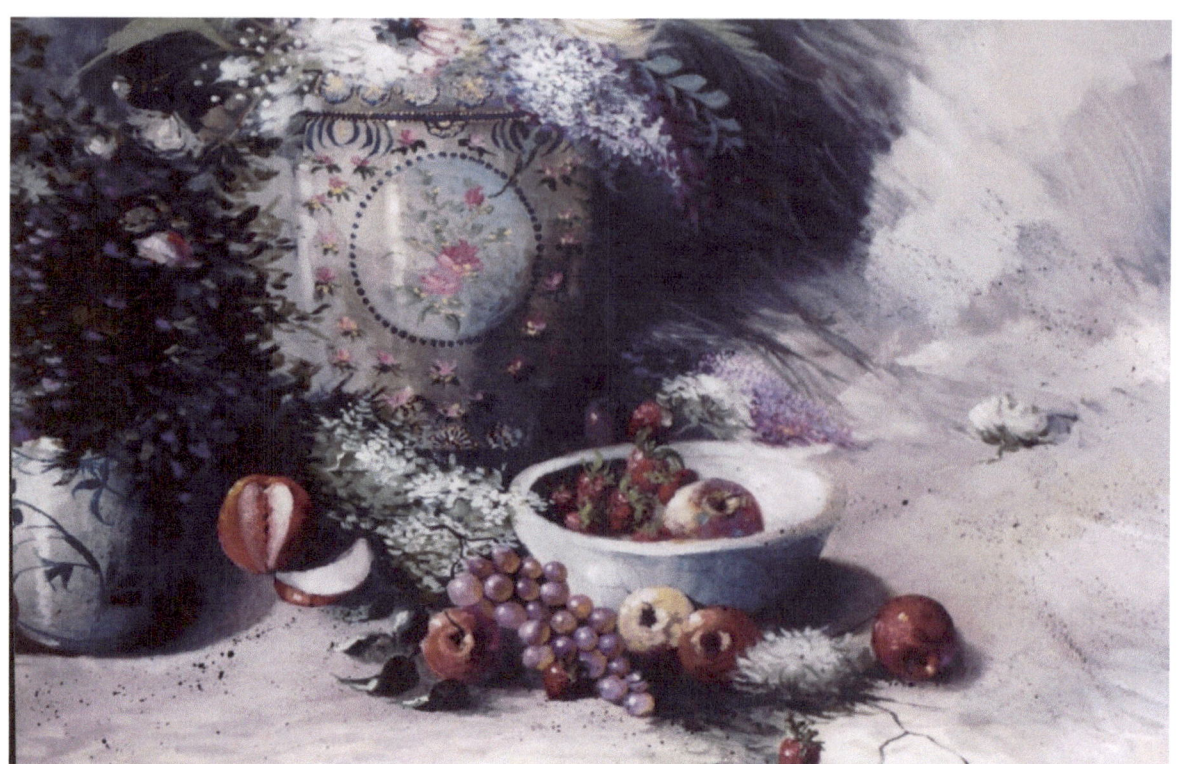

Holiday Bouquet with Still Life
30x40

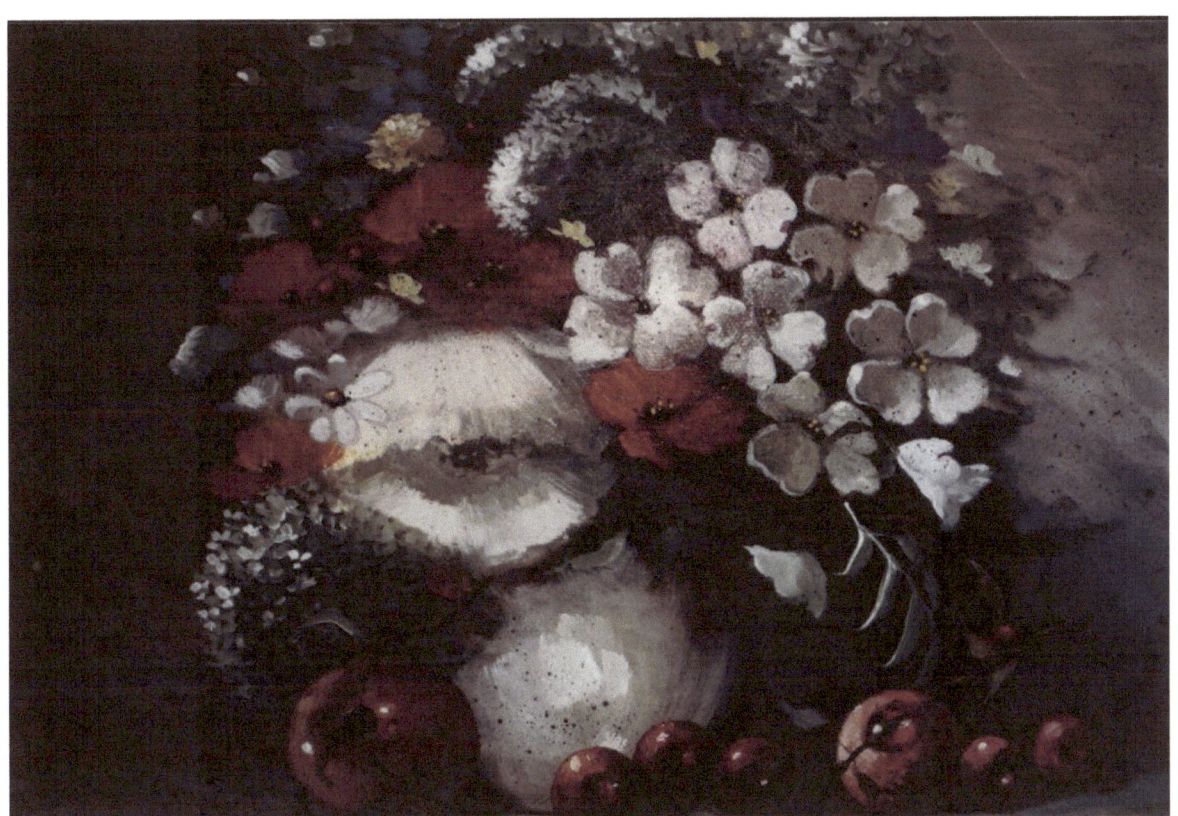

Bouquet w/Dogwood..

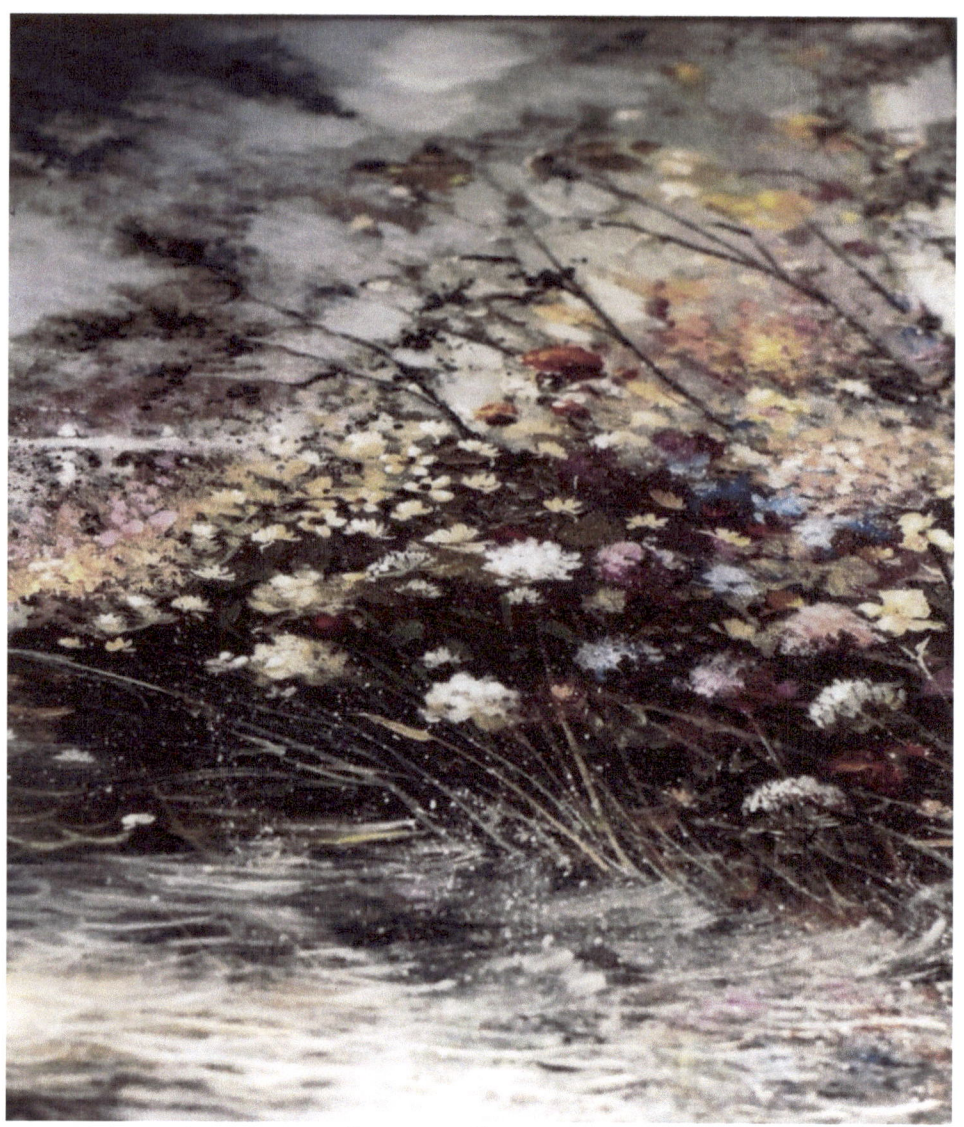

My Dads Hydrangea's - 2

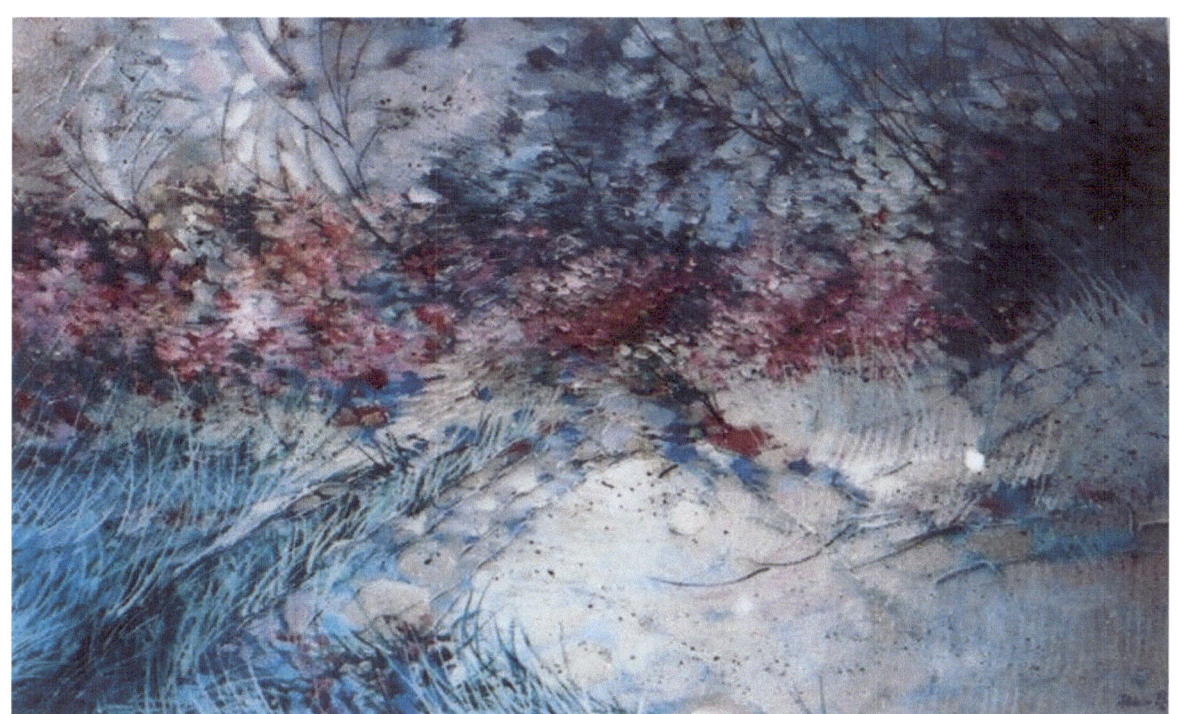

Large Paper Piece –

Azaleas in full bloom

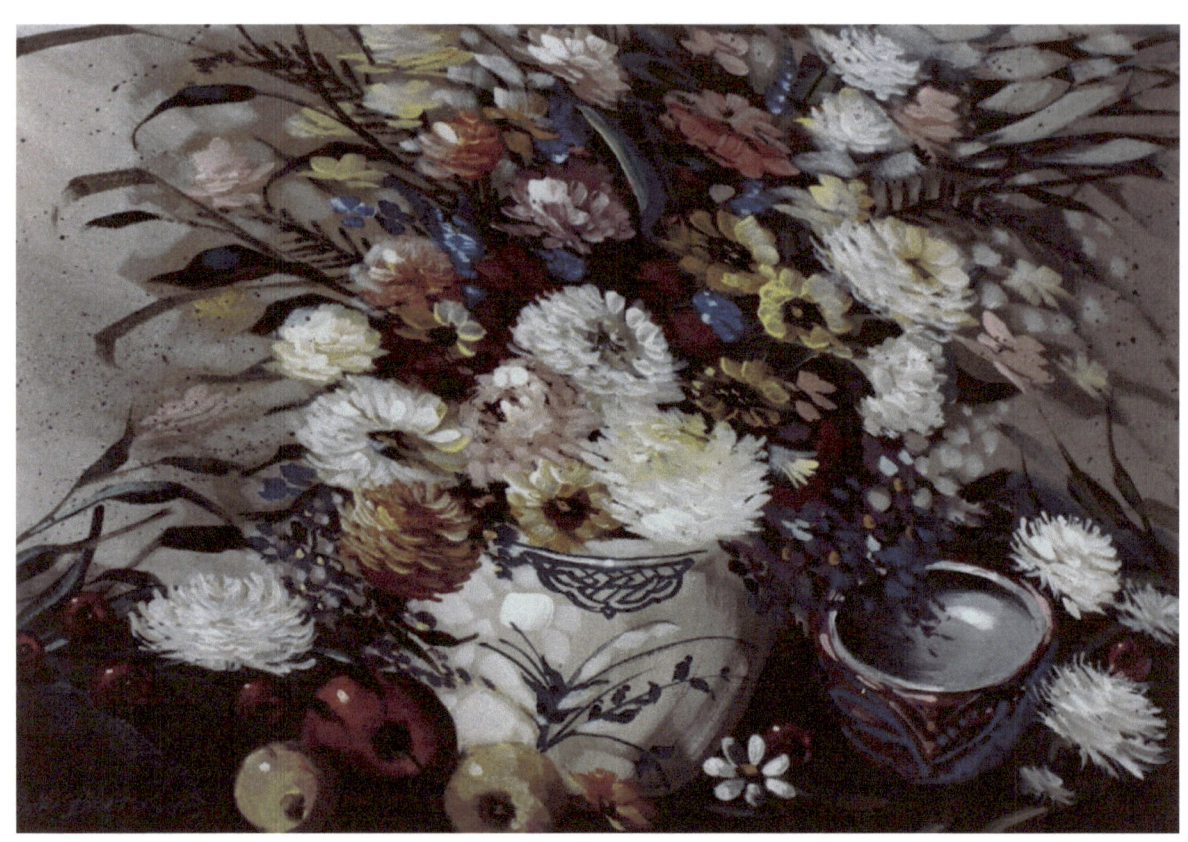

Potpourri of Flowers

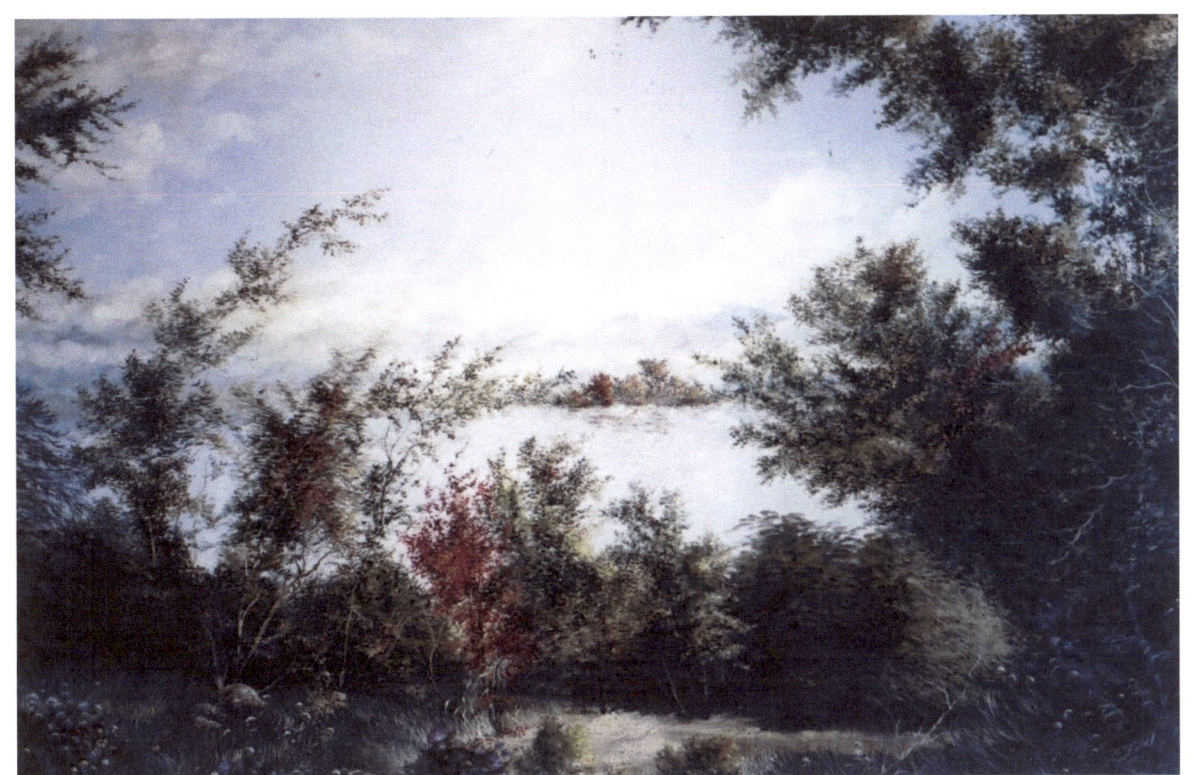

Overlook above the cove…

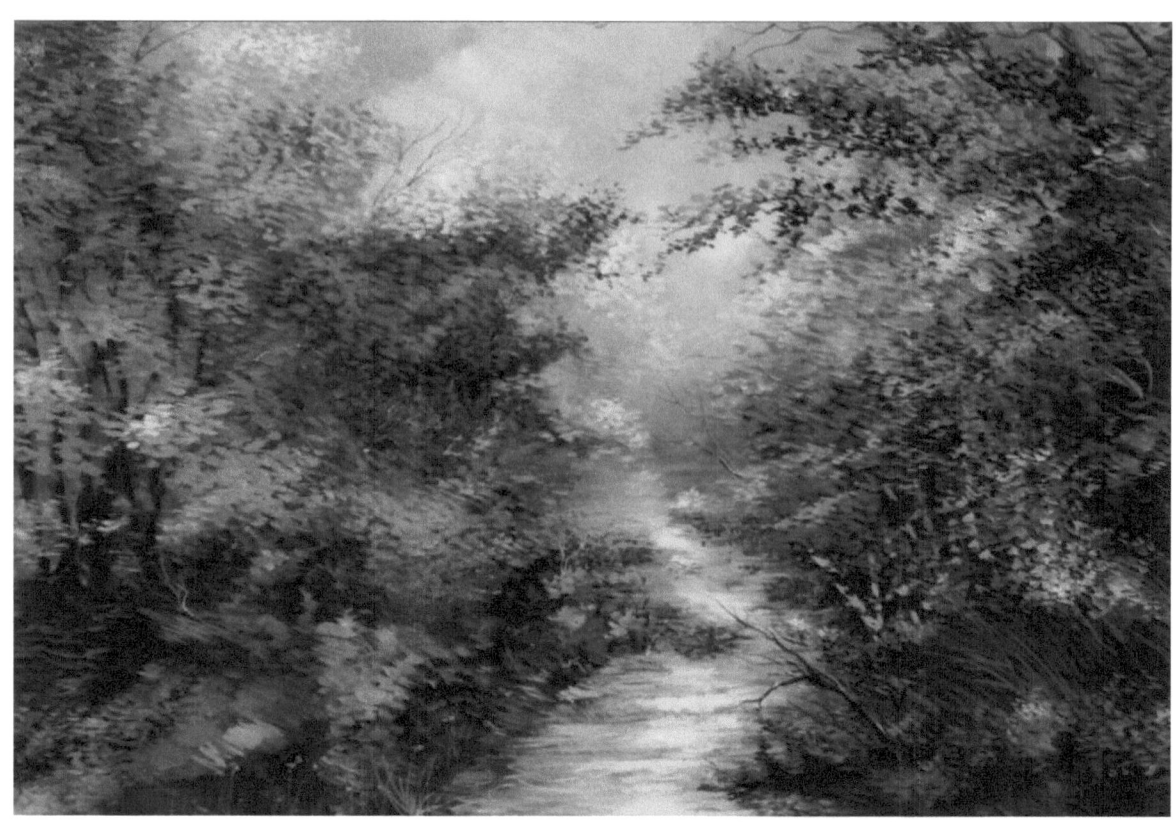

Spring on Timpson's Creek

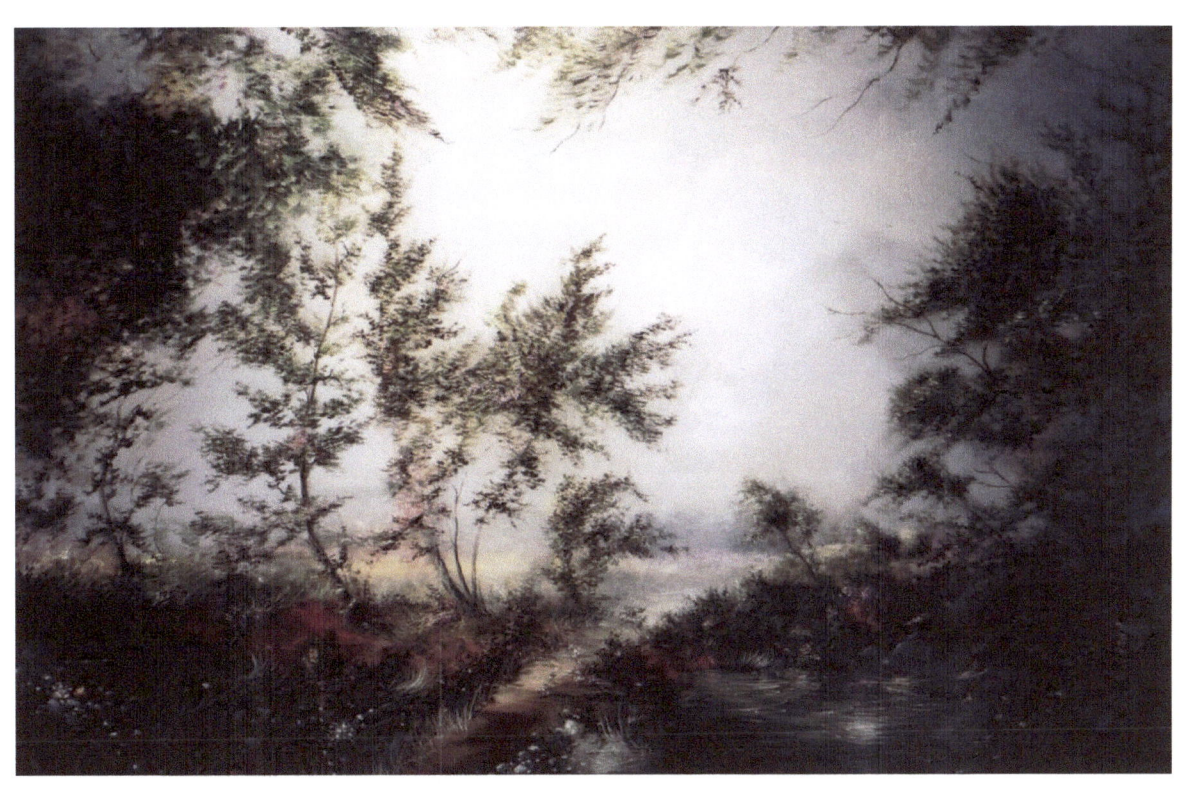

Nacoochee Valley

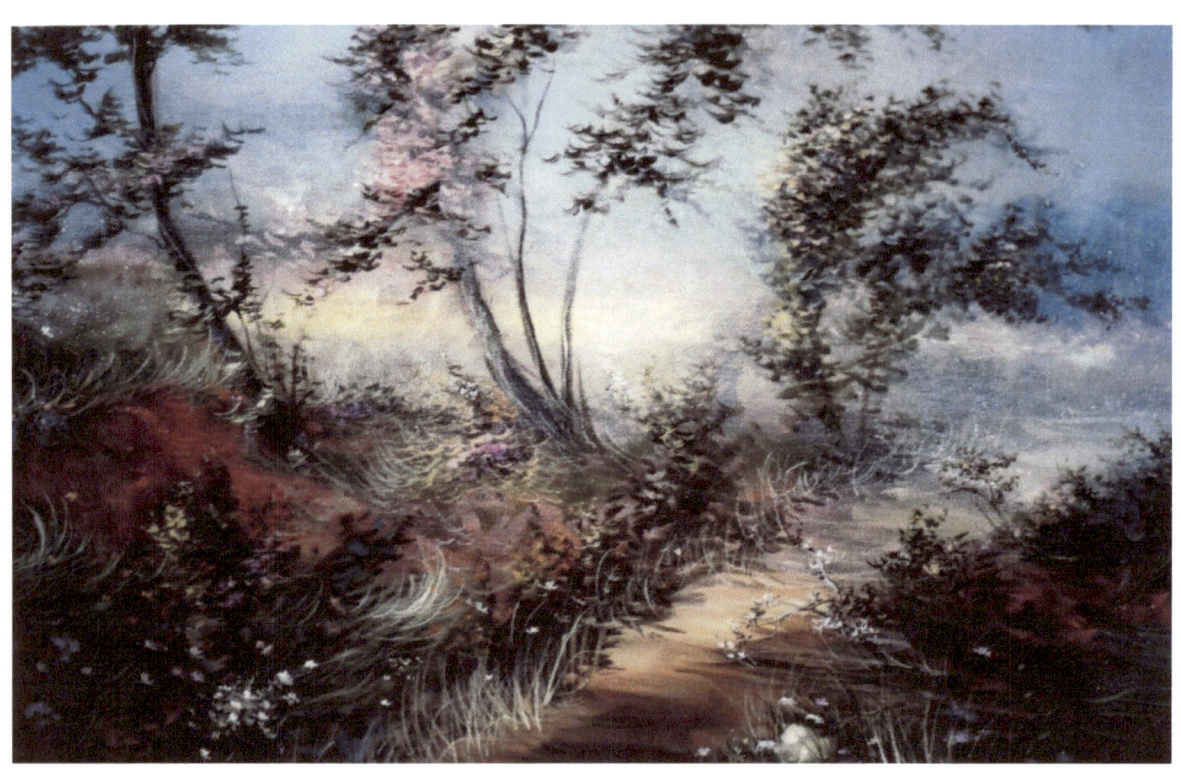

2nd Detail - Nacoochee Valley

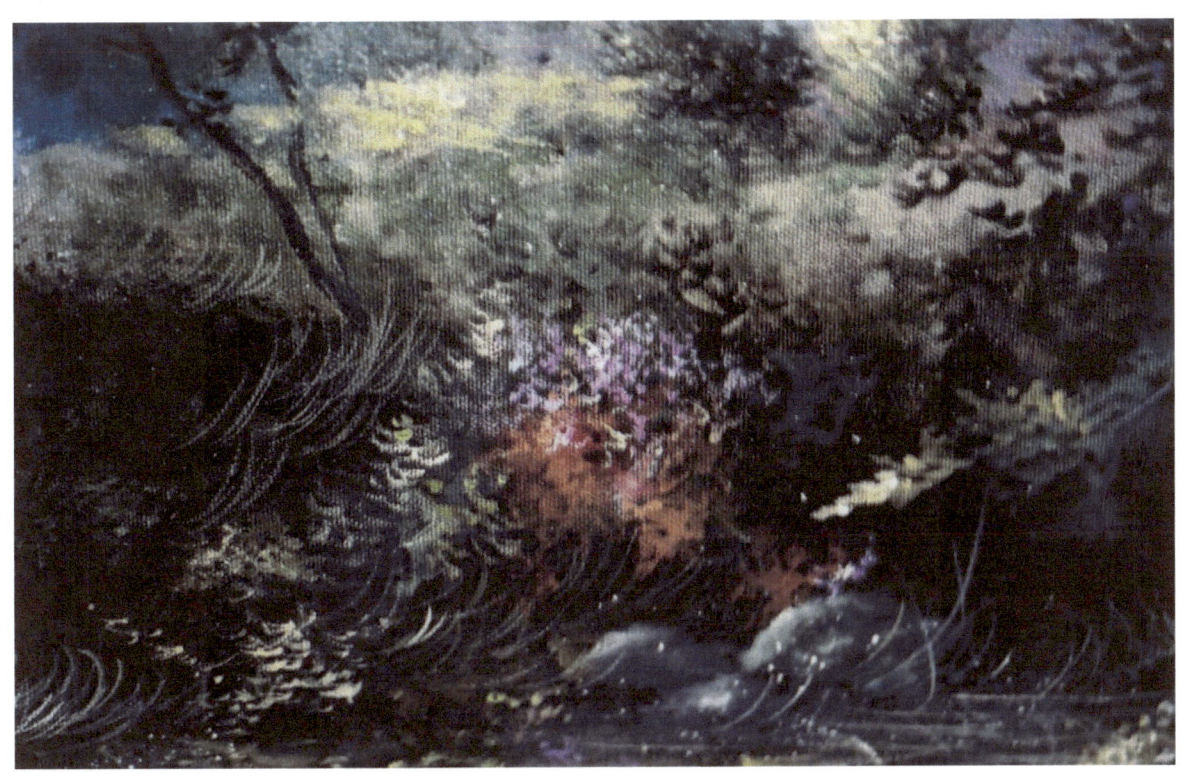

more detail - Nacoochee Valley

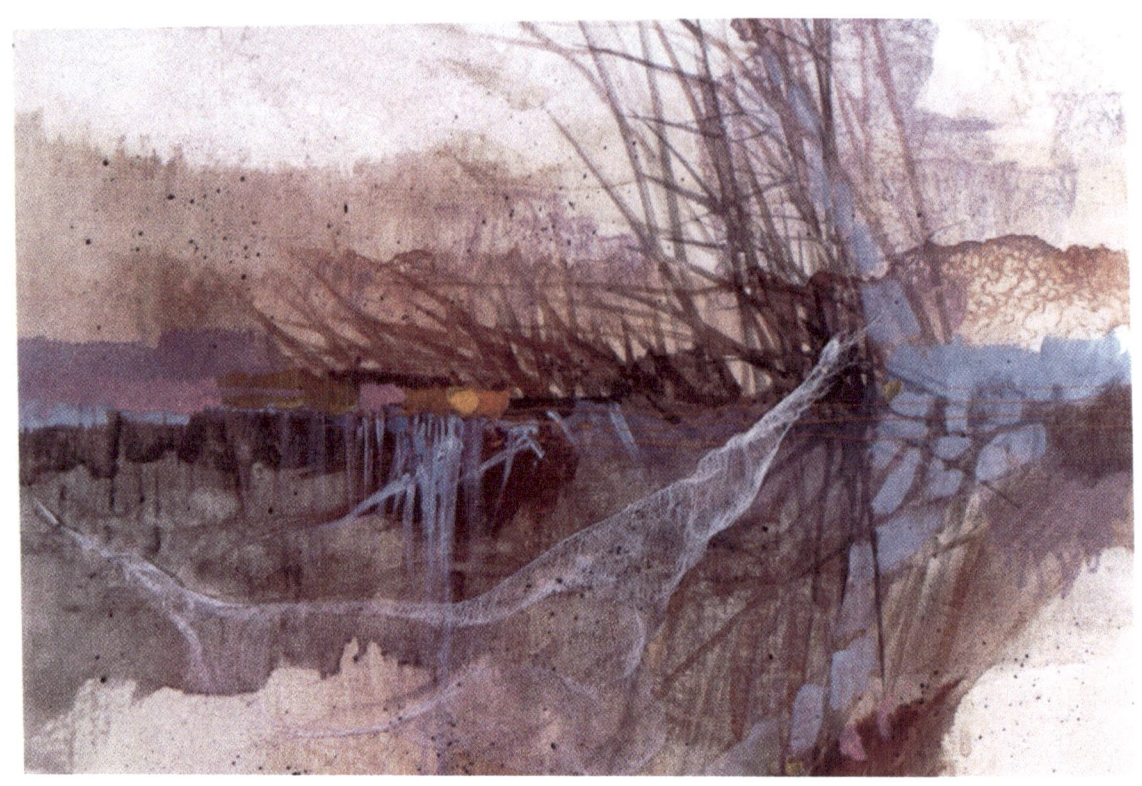

The Pond

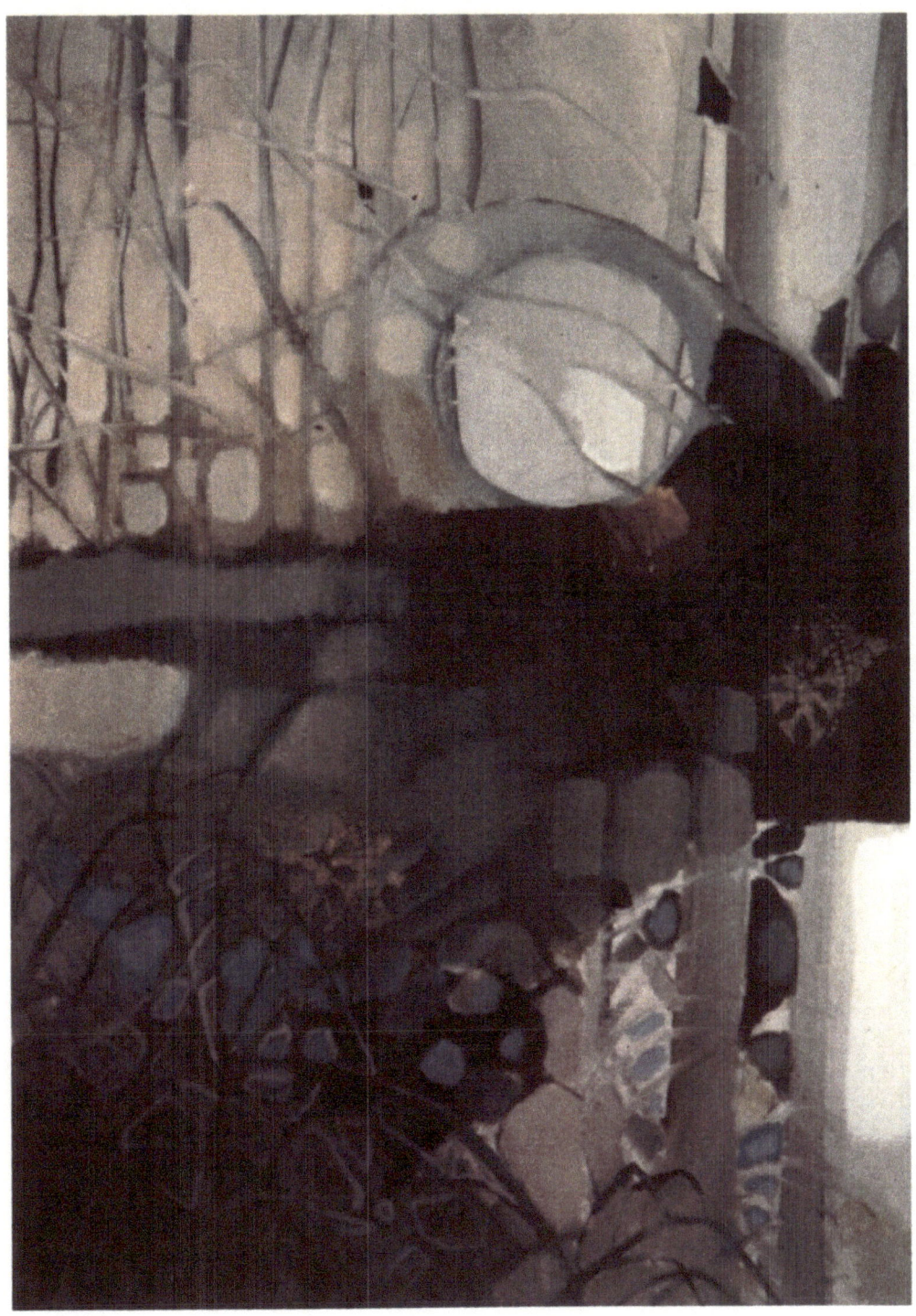

Patio

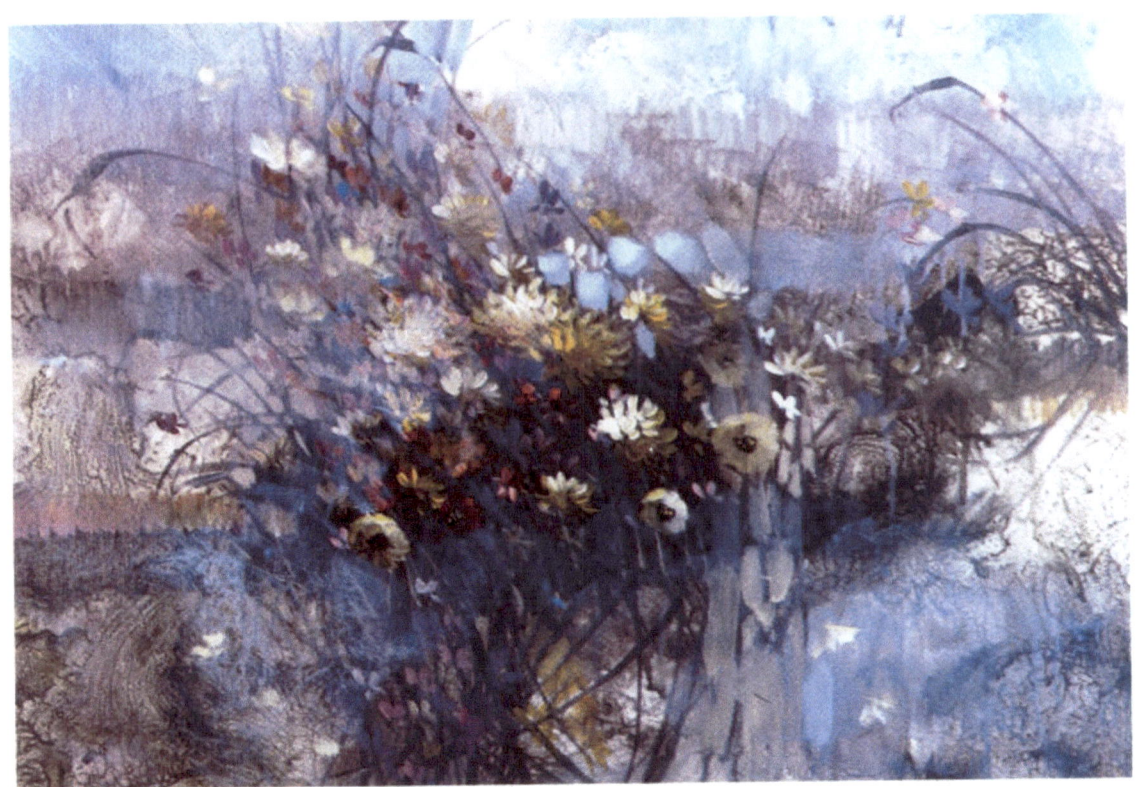

Wild Garden

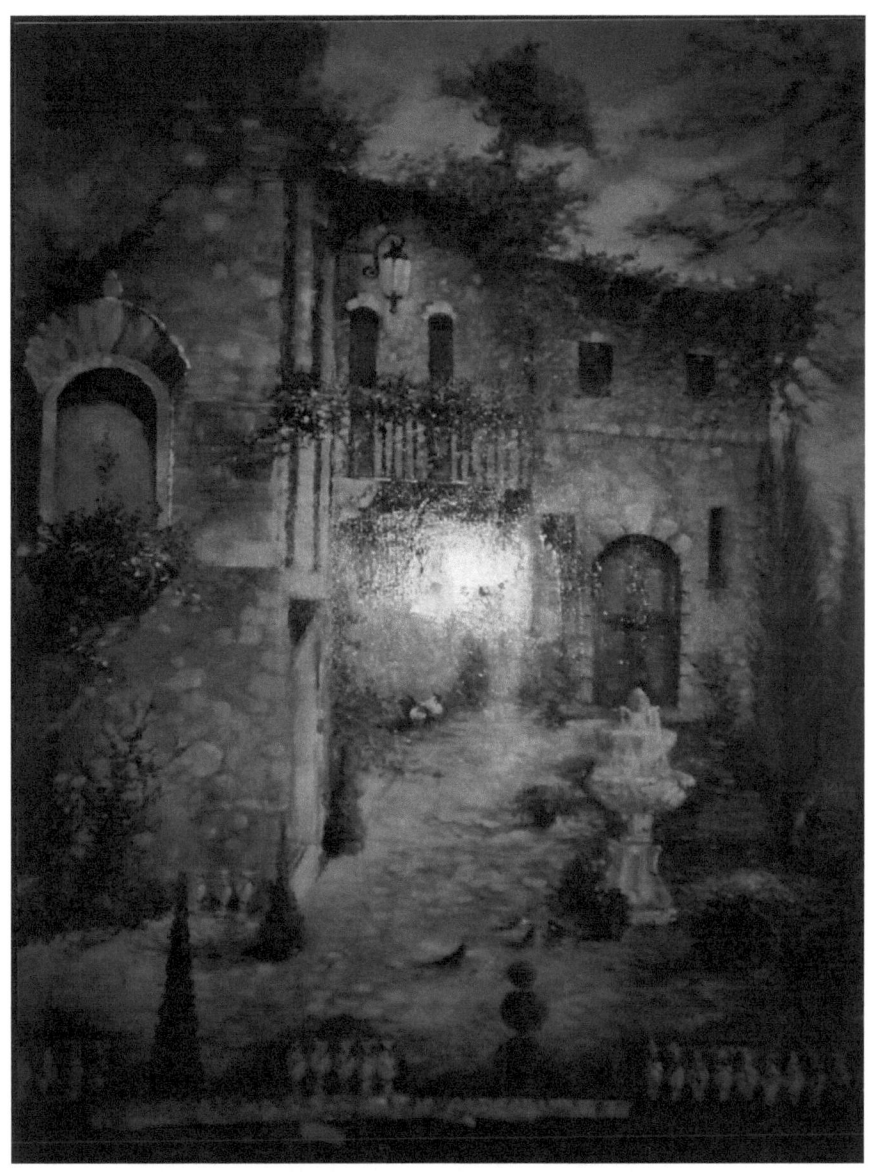

Tuscany

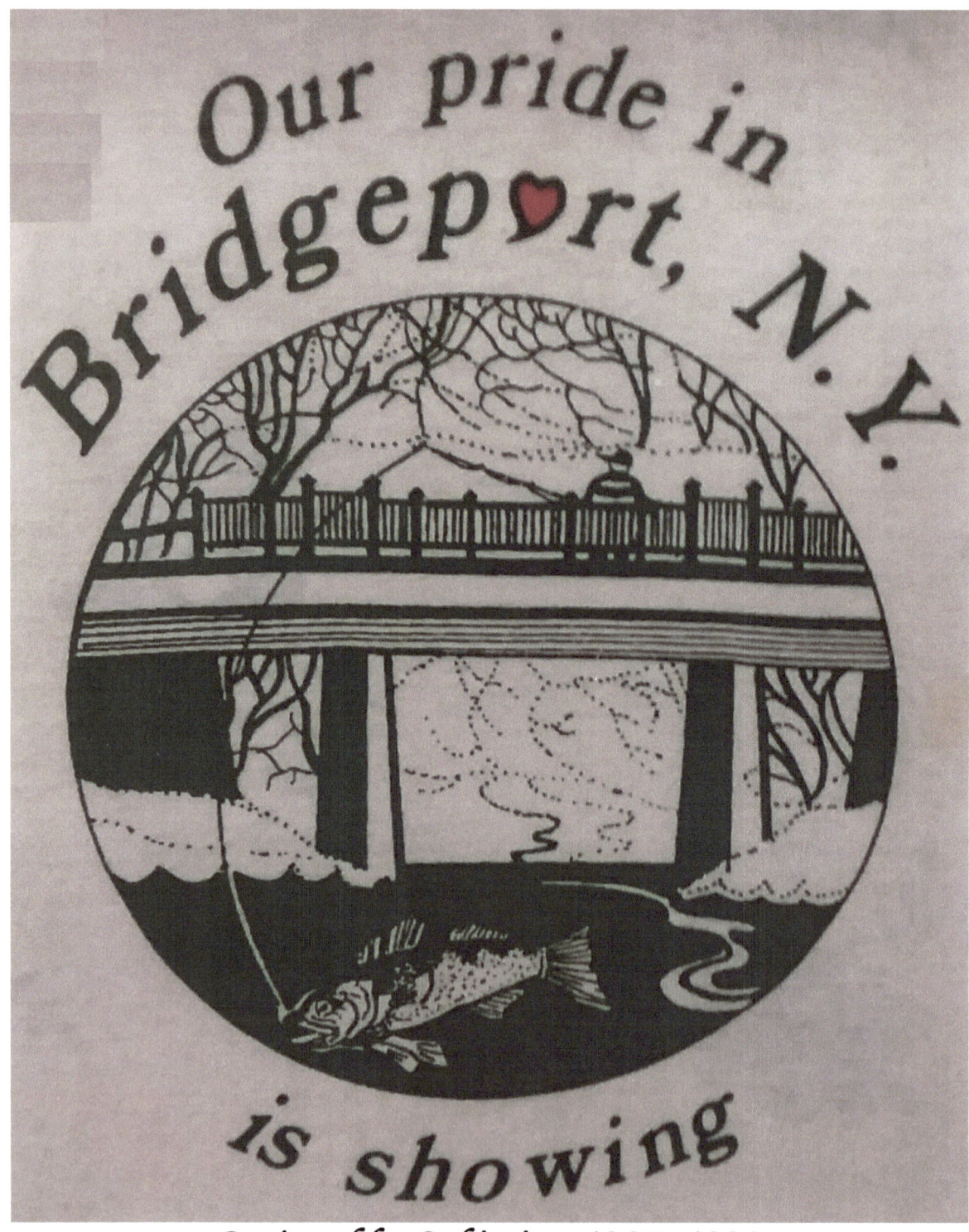

Designed by Robin in ~1987~1990.

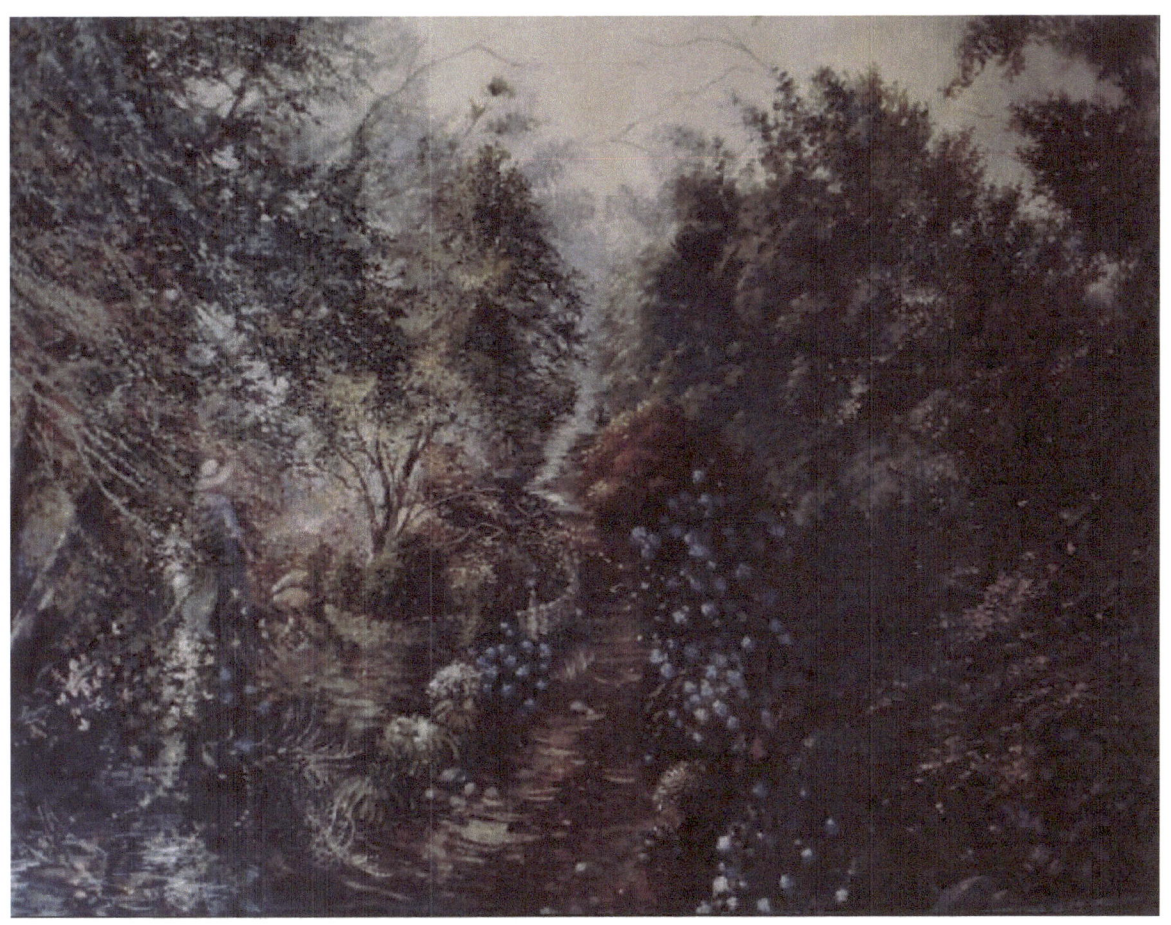

Hydrangeas by the Lake

2017 CFUMC Arts Festival "Grand Prize and Audience Choice Award" [1]

[1] CFUMC Arts Festival 2017 http://artsfestivalcfumc.com/2017-professional-awards/

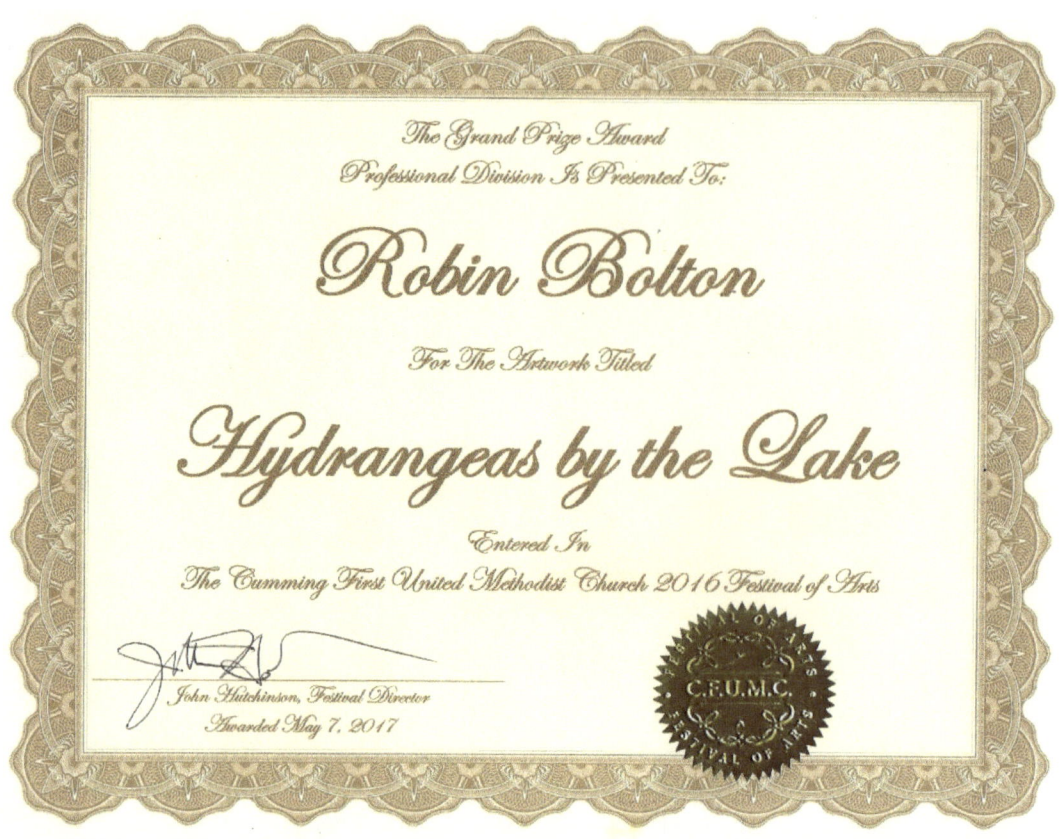

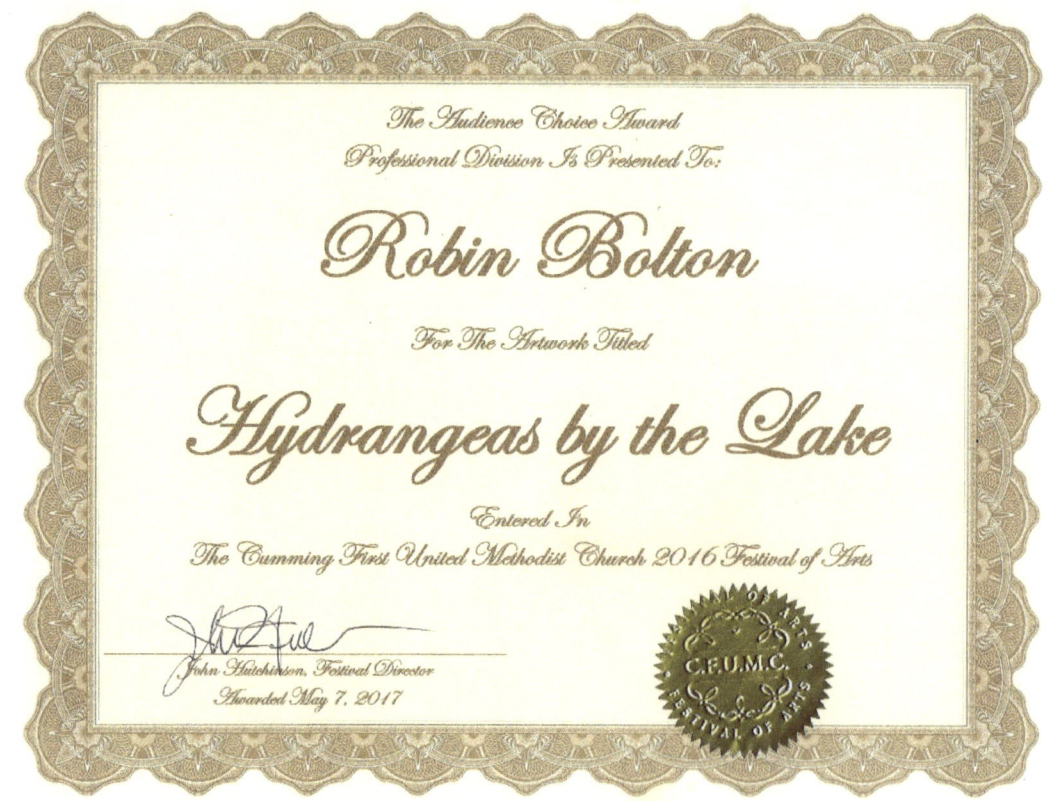

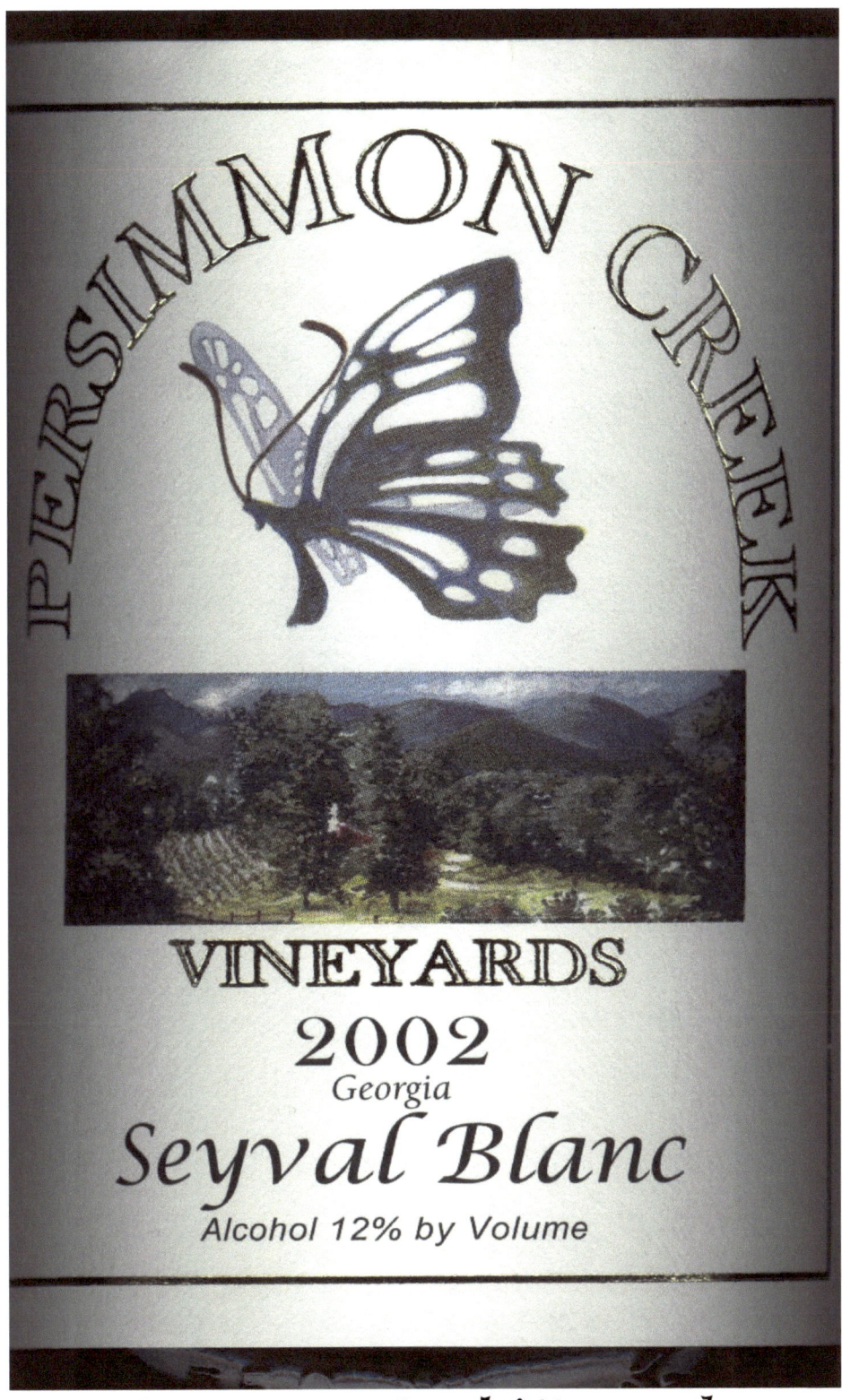

Persimmon Creek Vineyards

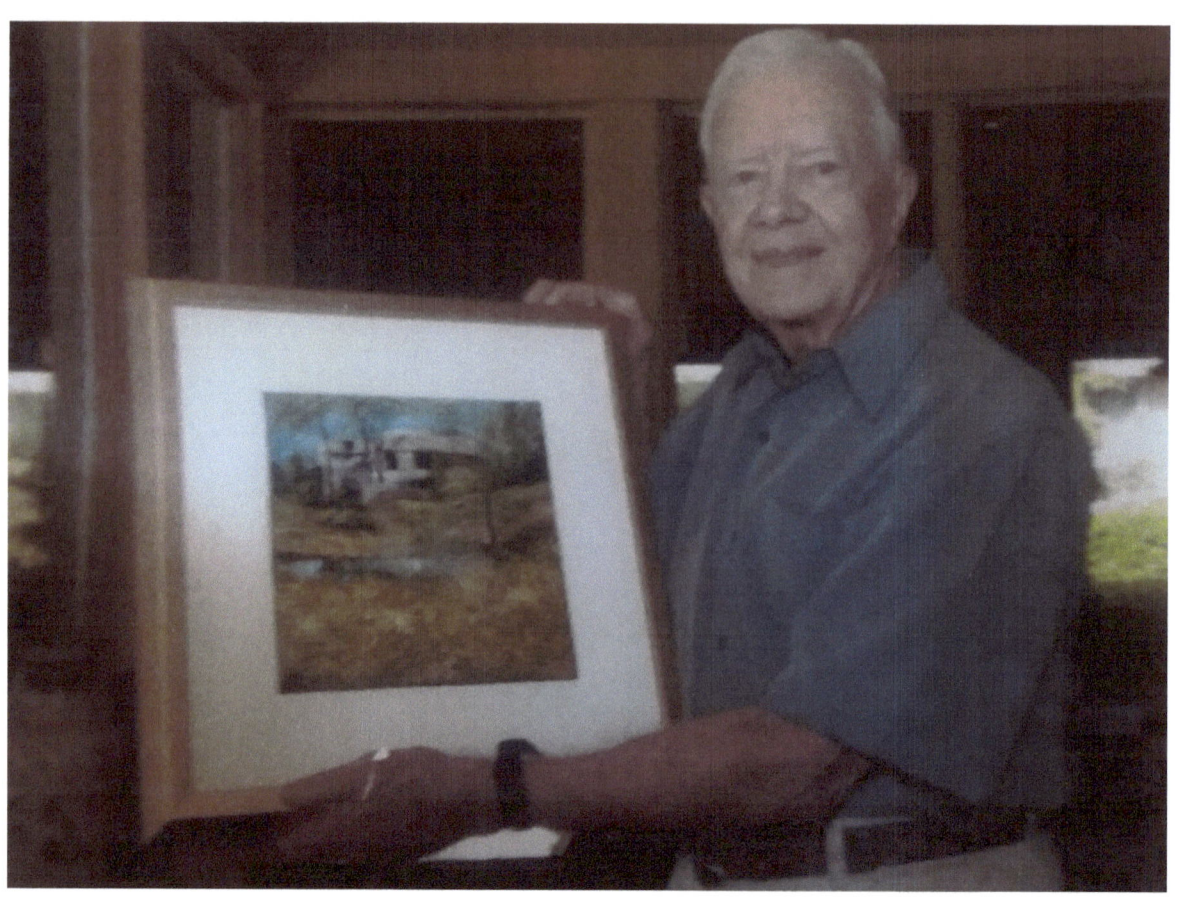

Jimmy Carter with Carter Center Painting

About the Artist

"Mrs. Bolton received her BFA degree from the University of Georgia and later worked for advertising firms in Atlanta and Chicago."

"The artist has received numerous awards in the Cooperstown National Juried Exhibitions and the Binghampton Arena National Juried Exhibitions and is represented in a large number of public and private collections."

"Robin Bolton has more than 10 solo exhibitions to her credit and has exhibited in numerous juried shows including those at the Everson Museum of Art in Syracuse and the Munson-William-Proctor Institute in Utica, New York."

"Robin has given many lectures and demonstrations throughout New York including The Rochester Memorial Art Gallery, Rochester, New York and the Arnot Art Museum, Elmira, New York.

On the Wall

* 10 Paintings in the IBM Collection
* President and Mrs. Jimmy Carter's Collection
* Miss Lillian Carter's Collection
* Capital Building – Atlanta, GA

Awards

* First Prize in Painting – Cooperstown National Juried
* First Prize in Painting – Arena Nat'l Juried – Binghamton, NY
* Henry Mallory Memorial Award – Cooperstown National
* Eugene Roma, Purchase Award – Arena National Juried
* The Louis H. Picciano Purchase Award – Arena National Juried
* Grand Prize and Audience Choice Award – CFUMC Arts Festival 2017

Robin J. Bolton
....
is a member in good standing
of the
COOPERSTOWN ART ASSOCIATION, Inc.

Membership expires **JUN 1 1977**

Henry S. F. Cooper
....
                                                    Treasurer

Liverpool Arts & Crafts Guild

Liverpool, New York
Organized ~ 1972

ROBIN BOLTON

is a member in good standing

Date *Feb 74*   Treasurer *Ben Surrett*

Judges Panel

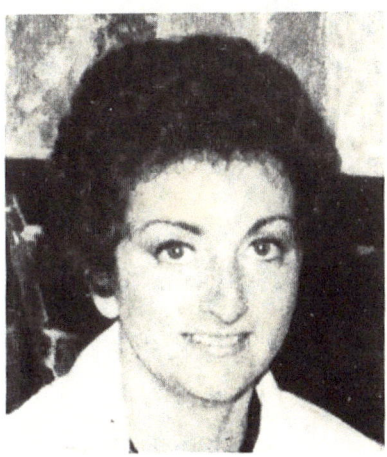

ROBIN BOLTON

n talent and

c.

ng tap, jazz,

all over the

elevision, as
unity groups

per National

eacher Now

ard of Suc-

Mrs. Bolton received her BFA degree from the University of Georgia and later worked for advertising firms in Atlanta and Chicago.

The artist has received numerous awards in recent Cooperstown National Juried Exhibitions and the Binghamton Area National Juried Exhibitions and is represented in a large number of public and private collections.

Robin Bolton has more than 10 solo exhibitions to her credit and has exhibited in numerous juried shows including those at the Everson Museum of Art in Syracuse and the Munson-William-Proctor Institute in Utica, New York.

Robin has given many lectures and demonstrations throughout New York including The Rochester Memorial Art Gallery, Rochester, New York and the Arnot Art Museum, Elmira, New York.

Judge @ Lehigh Acres, Florida

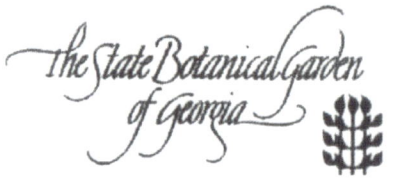

The University of Georgia
2450 South Milledge Ave.
Athens, Ga 30602
www.uqa.edu/botgarden

**You are invited to attend an
exhibit by
Robin Ricketson Bolton**

MarquisWho'sWho in American Art
IBM Corporation - New York
Mobile Oil Corporation - Rochester, NY
Farash Corporation - Rochester, NY
Cooperstown Nat'l, First Prize,
Cooperstown, NY Federated Hall,
Tallulah Falls School, GA

**September 12, 2004
2:00 - 4:00pm**

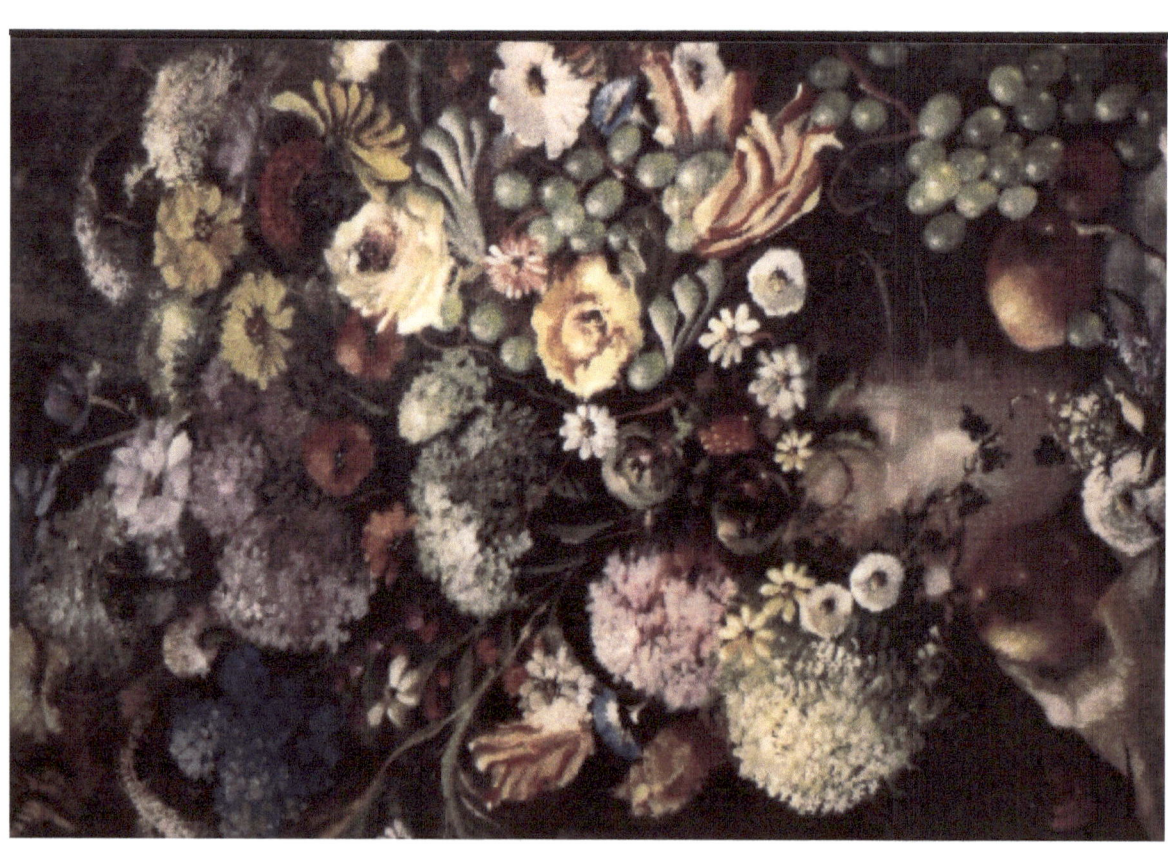

Sprayberry High School Collage (*1971-2015)

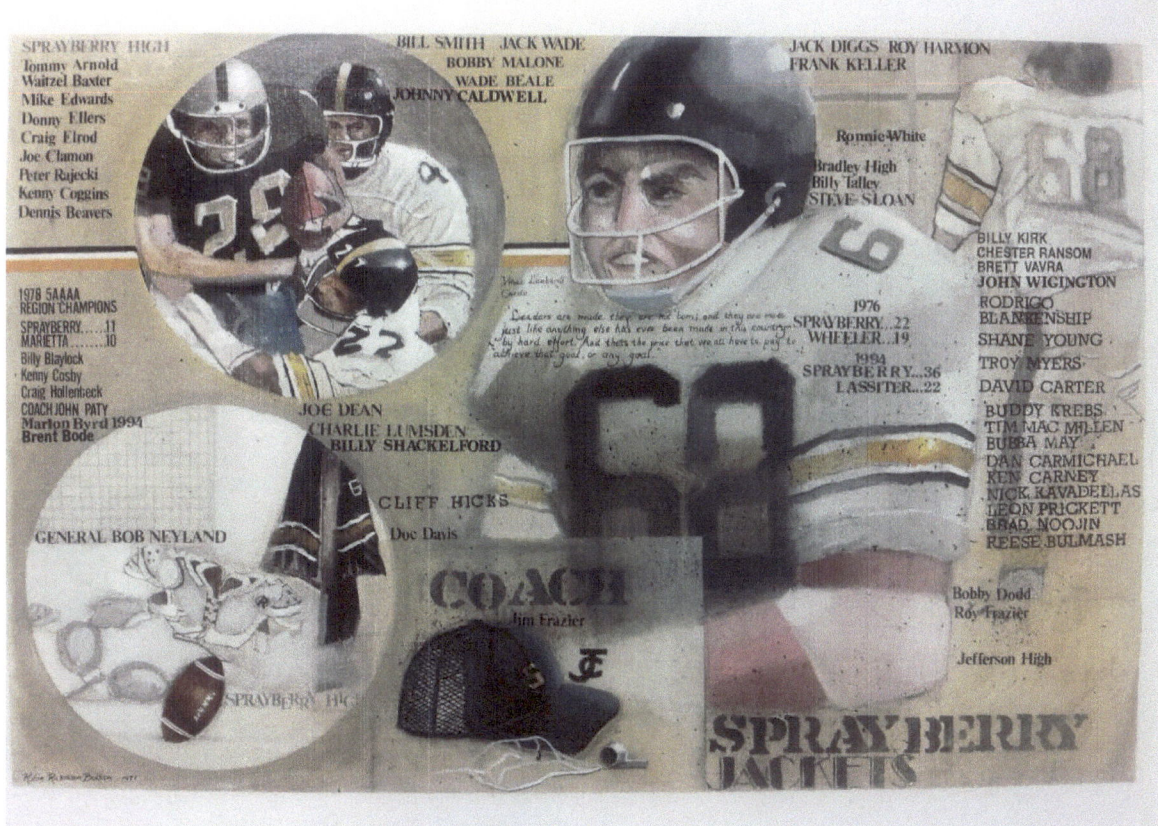

*Longest consecutive period of work on a single Painting – 1971-2014

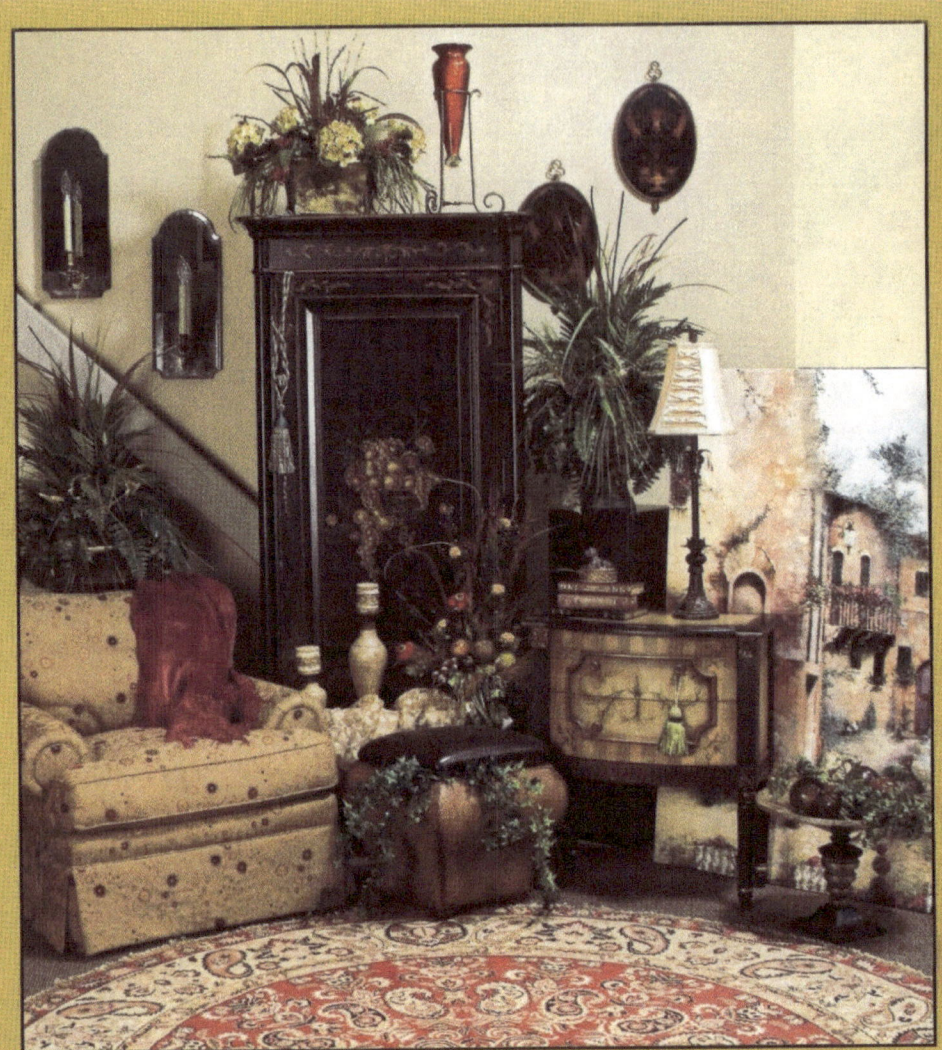
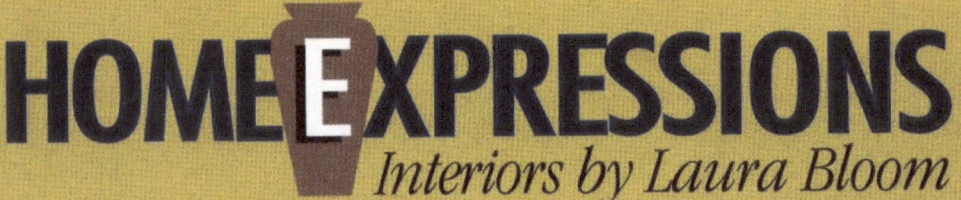
THE ART OF ROBIN BOLTON – FIRST EDITION

CFUMC
Festival of Arts

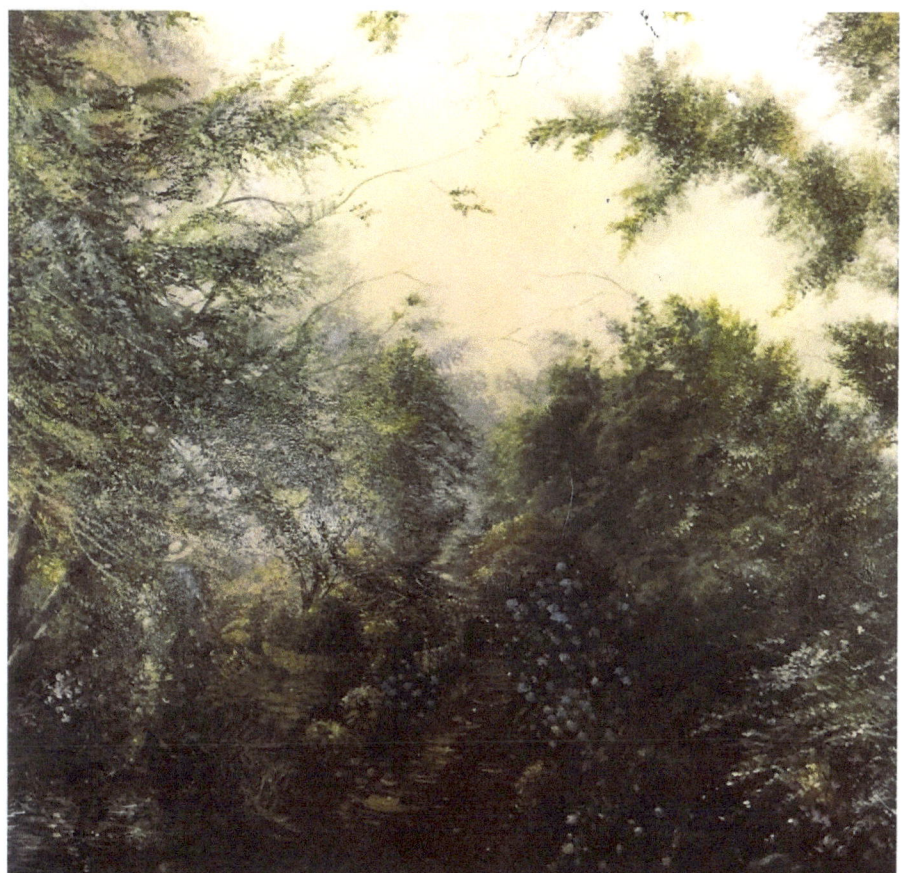

Hydrangeas by the Lake—by Robin Bolton—2017 Grand Prize & Audience Choice Winner

April 15 - April 28, 2018

Cumming First United Methodist Church
770 Canton Hwy * Cumming, GA 30040 * www.cfumcga.com

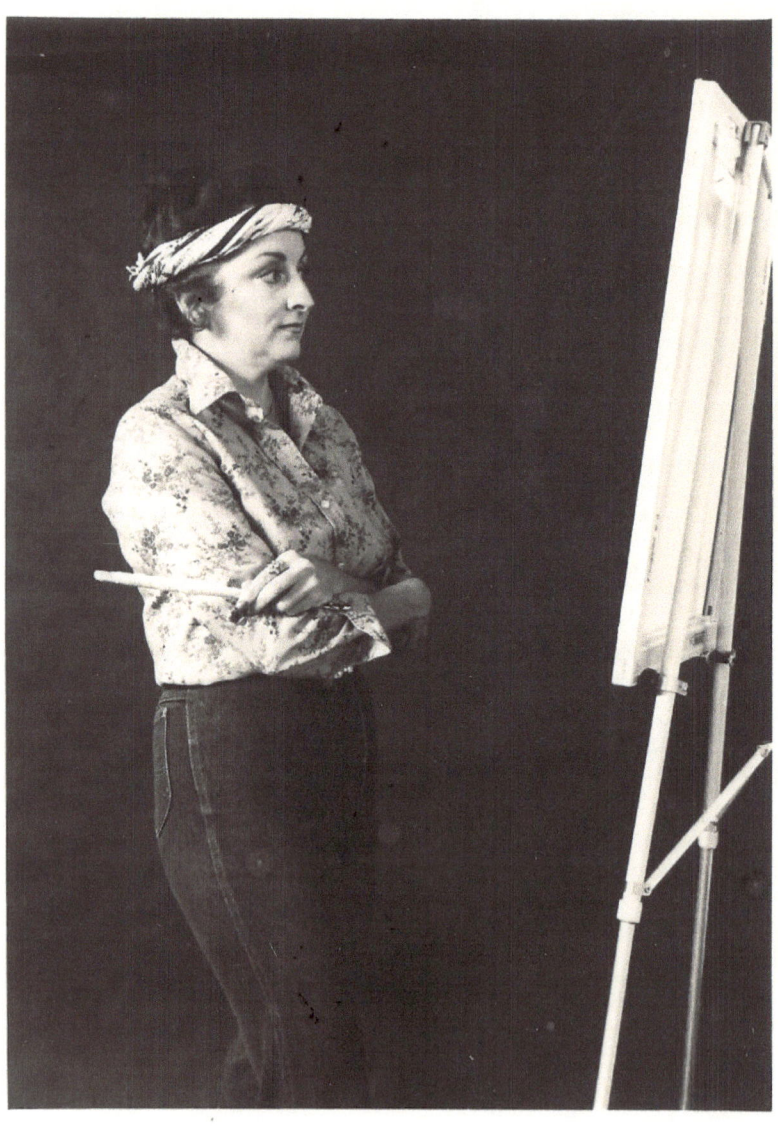

Painting

by

Robin Bolton   7720 Treeline Dr.
Phone 652-3250   Liverpool, New York, 13088
Liverpool Arts & Crafts Guild